AF539261

PICTURES THAT TALK

Selected Works by Tad Savinar

LINDA TESNER

Ronna and Eric Hoffman Gallery of Contemporary Art
Lewis & Clark College
Portland, Oregon

Pictures that Talk is published by the Ronna and Eric Hoffman Gallery of Contemporary Art, Lewis & Clark College
0615 S. W. Palatine Hill Road
Portland, Oregon 97219

ISBN: 9780692762196
Library of Congress Control Number: 2016954476

Photography Credits
In Pursuit of Joy, *Patterns*, and *H5N1 Virus Central Library Distribution Pad* by Bill Bachhuber. Photography for other plates by Aaron Johanson, except where noted.

Available through:
ARTBOOK | D.A.P.
155 6th Avenue, 2nd Floor
New York, NY 10013
www.artbook.com

Produced by Lucia | Marquand, Seattle
www.luciamarquand.com

Designed by Ryan Polich
Edited by Carolyn Vaughan
Typeset in Adobe Text Pro by Maggie Lee
Proofread by Barbara Bowen
Color management by iocolor, Seattle
Printed and bound in China by C&C Offset Printing Co., Ltd.

Introduction 6

Fourteen Works 11

Pictures that Talk 41

Biography 69

Artist's Acknowledgments 70

Director's Acknowledgments 71

Introduction

Tad Savinar and I had multiple discussions about how we hoped this book might be used by the reader. There were some physical considerations—we wanted a book that would feel good in the hand, whose dimensions and paper-feel were pleasurable and inviting. A page layout and type font conducive to reading. Not too many plates—more words than pictures: only fourteen works are reproduced and discussed, out of more than forty-four years of Savinar's studio practice. The works of art under consideration are reproduced at the beginning of the book. Not that Savinar and I hoped to turn art-book convention on its ear; rather, we wanted to start at the beginning: with the artwork. What follows is an essay about those works, which the artist and I feel are emblematic of his oeuvre. Our highest hope is that the experience of the book—looking, reading, digesting—will simulate the experience of visiting a small, tightly curated exhibition, then being able to sit down over coffee with the curator for a conversation.

Savinar rarely signs his work on the face; there is no signature or other flourish that immediately identifies the artist. Typical of his preeminent thoughtfulness and attention to detail, Savinar feels that a signature indicates that the work is now finished and ready to leave the studio for public consumption. That the artist's designation says to the viewer, "You are not a part of this process." Herein lies a critical aspect of Savinar's work, one that is important to remember while viewing it. Savinar's art—a print, a sculpture, a book—is *always* an invitation to the viewer to join him in a dialogue about the subject of the piece, wherever that might lead. It is a bit as if each work by Savinar is the beginning of an exquisite corpse game, in which the viewers' responses ultimately close the circle in the art experience.

In 1999 Terri Hopkins, director of Marylhurst University's The Art Gym, organized a mid-career survey of Savinar's work, *Excerpts from a Conversation 1976–1999*, with an accompanying catalogue of the same name. In January 2017 I organized *youniverse—past, present, future: Selected Works by Tad Savinar from the Jordan D. Schnitzer Collection* at the Ronna and Eric Hoffman Gallery of Contemporary Art, Lewis & Clark College. Drawing almost exclusively from the extensive collection of Jordan D. Schnitzer and from the artist himself, *youniverse* focused on two bodies of work. One included prints, paintings, and sculpture created between 1994 and 2011. The other portion contained works conceived in Florence, Italy, in 2014 and others that followed into 2016. This book is not an exhibition catalogue for the 2017 exhibition but an investigative discussion of the most significant fourteen works created by the artist between 1998 and 2016. Savinar's career is not linear in the sense of progressing from point A to point B. His creative output has been more cyclical or elliptical in nature, often orbiting or engaging in a specific subject matter or process only to come back twenty years later to revisit it with hindsight or an updated approach as society itself evolves . . . or doesn't.

Linda Tesner
Director
Ronna and Eric Hoffman Gallery of Contemporary Art, Lewis & Clark College
Portland, Oregon

I am interested in creating a dialogue between the work and the viewer. Not a one-way diatribe but a genuine back-and-forth conversation. In order to achieve this, I use the tool of beauty to bring the viewer closer, language to engage them, content that is relevant to their lives, and irony to soften the blow.

Tad Savinar

FOURTEEN WORKS

IN PURSUIT OF JOY
1998
Screenprint on fabric
81 × 47.5 inches
Collection of Jordan D. Schnitzer

Friendship

Time spent commiserating with
someone about how there is no joy.

Work

An activity through which
we try to verify our
own intelligence.

Marriage

A lifetime of sharing small
convoluted in-jokes.

Children

An investment in the future.

Community Service

The attempt to make things better
for the next guy
(who we all know could care less).

Being Alone

A reflective activity which places the
self in the context of what one is
experiencing (i.e. literature)
nature, genius, etc.)

WONDERS OF HEREDITY

2001

Screenprint on paper

14.5 × 32.5 inches

Collection of the Hampton Family

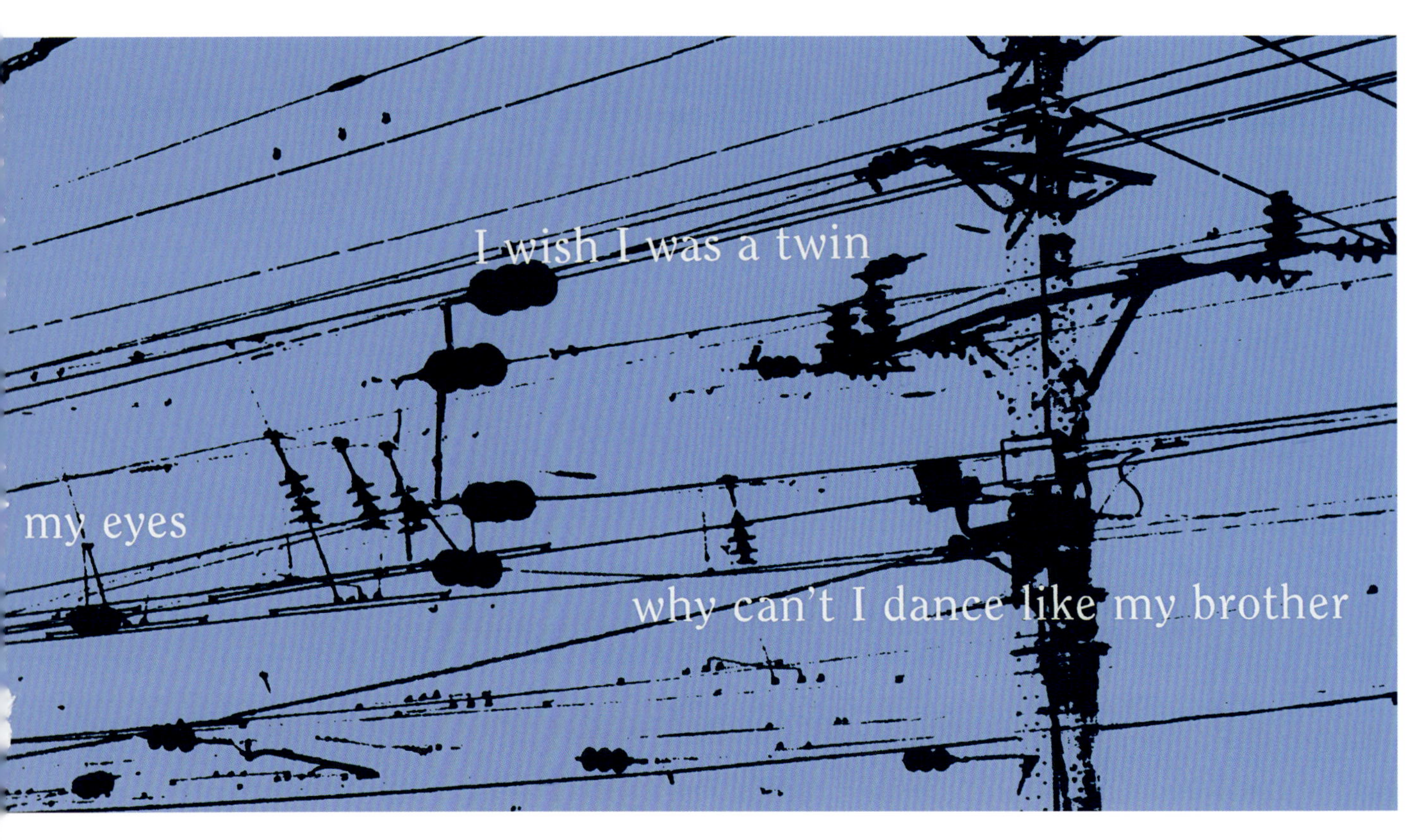
I wish I was a twin
my eyes
why can't I dance like my brother

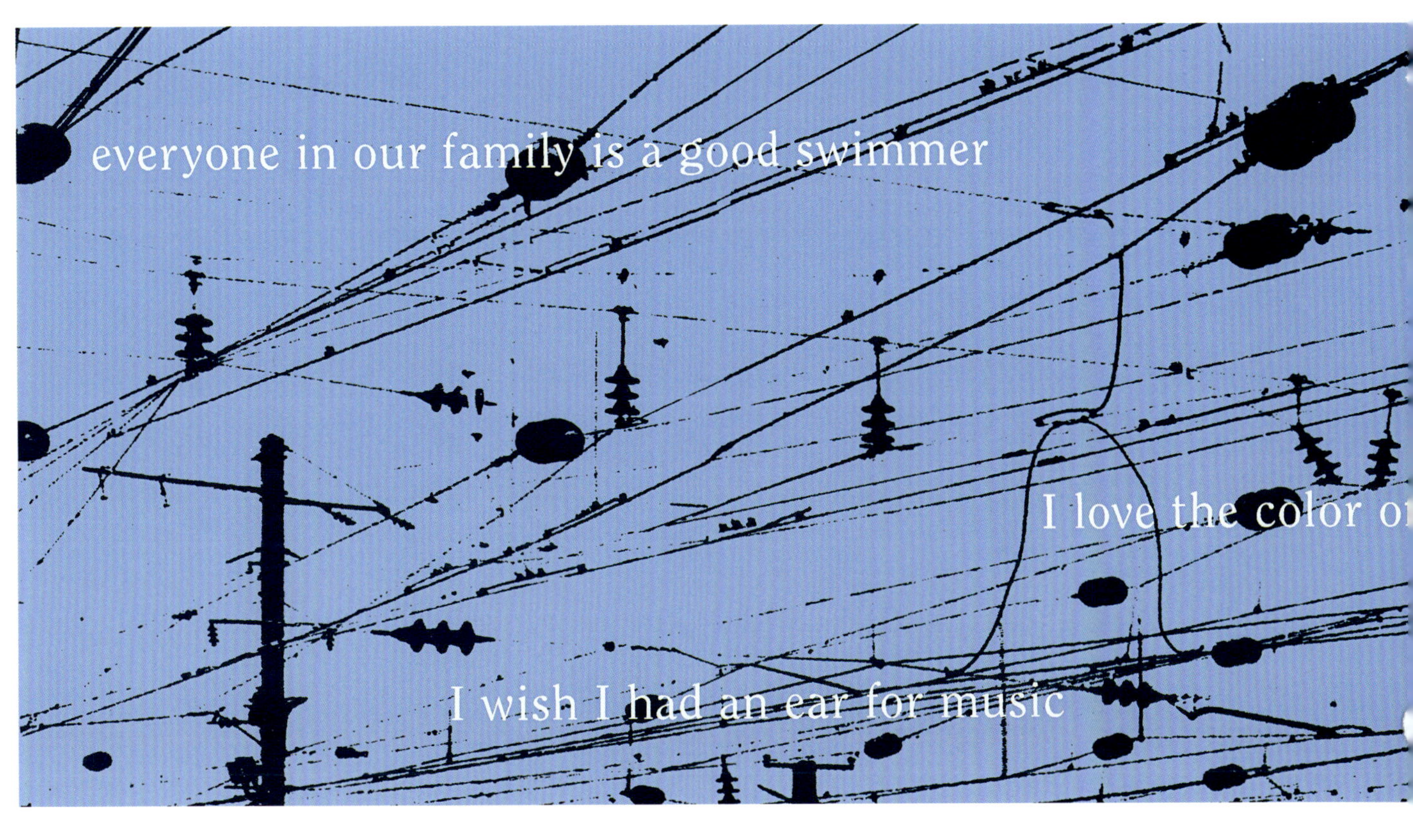
everyone in our family is a good swimmer
I love the color o
I wish I had an ear for music

PARENTS' DREAMS

1998

Screenprint on silk

Variable dimensions

Collection of the artist

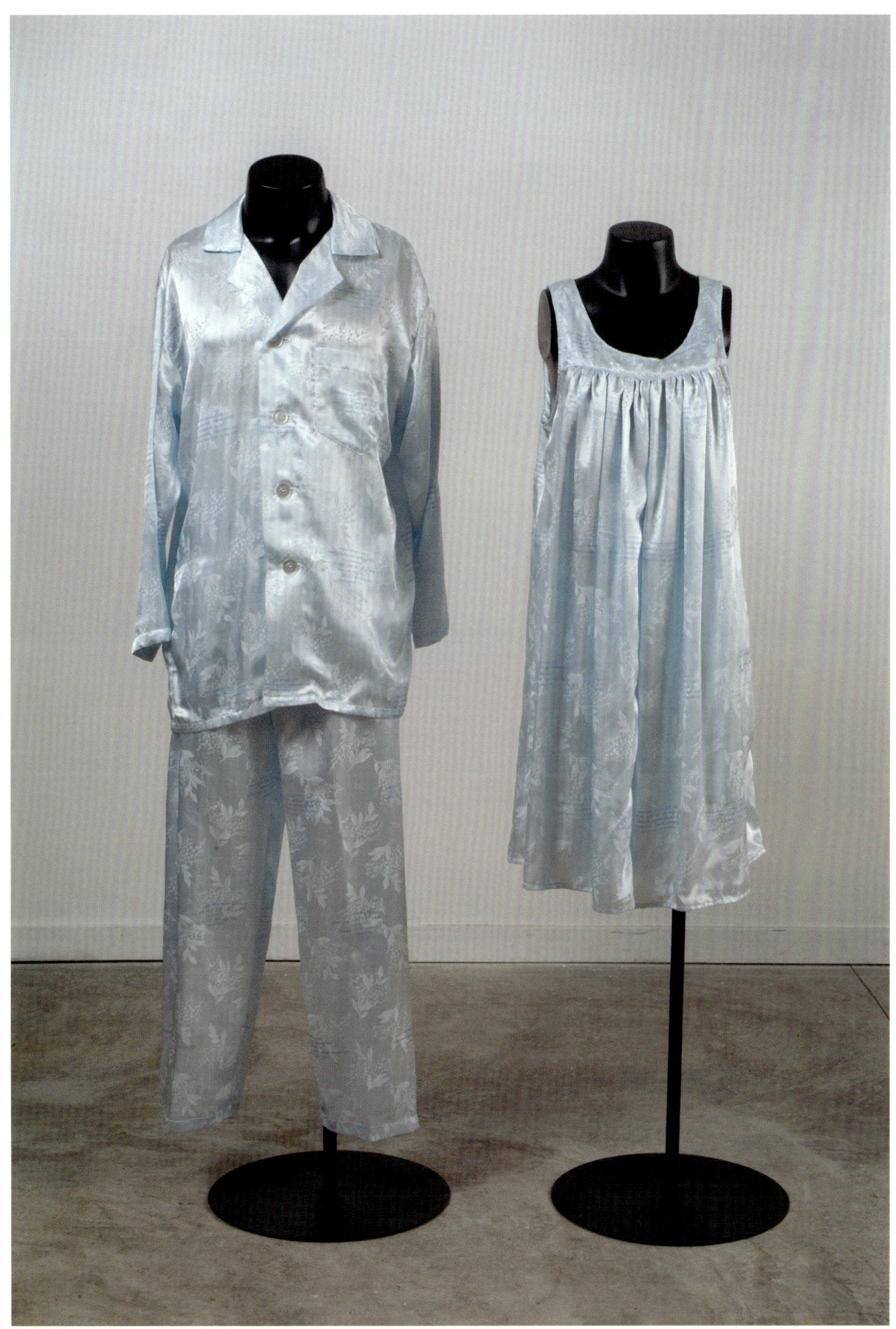

PATTERNS

2001

Screenprint on paper

39 × 61.5 inches

Collection of Jordan D. Schnitzer

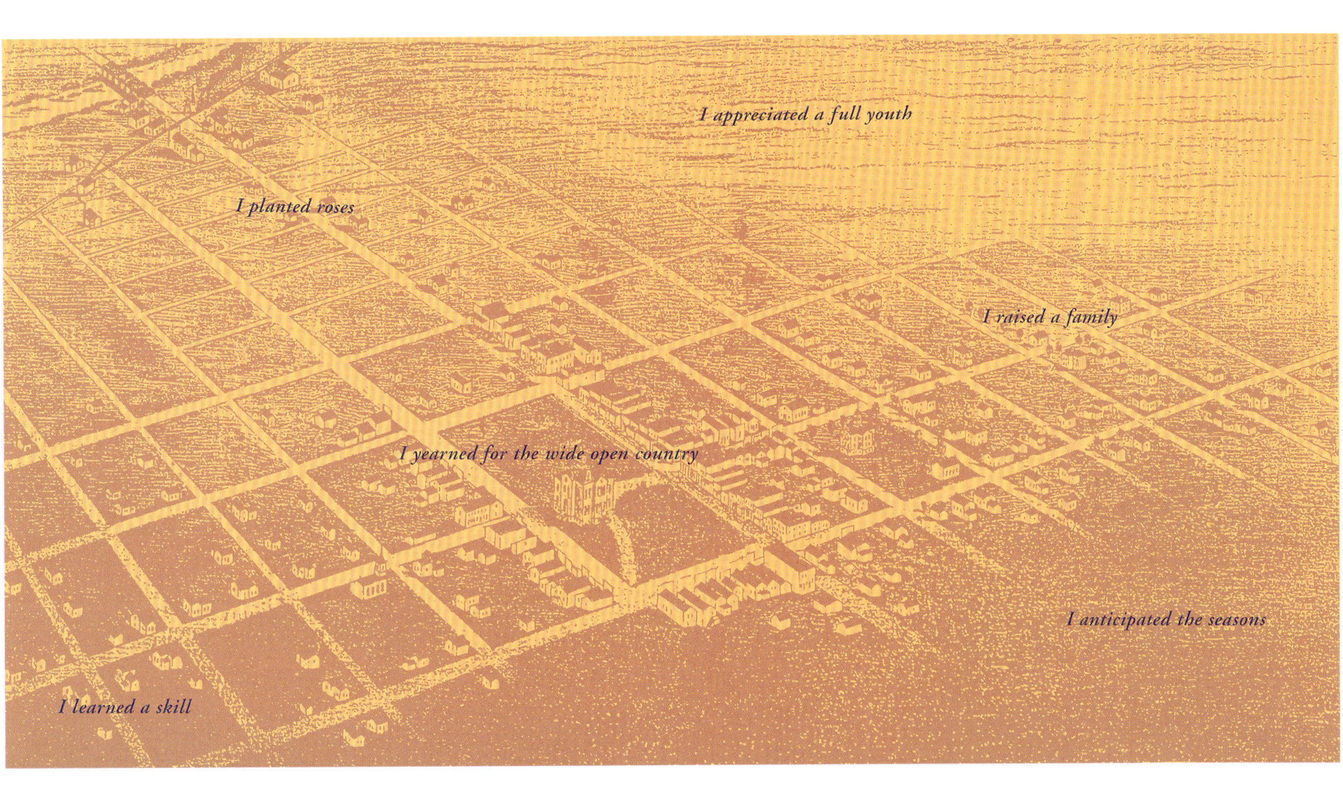
I appreciated a full youth
I planted roses
I raised a family
I yearned for the wide open country
I anticipated the seasons
I learned a skill

DEVELOPMENT

2006

Digitally carved wood

57.5 × 24 × 24 inches

Collection of the artist

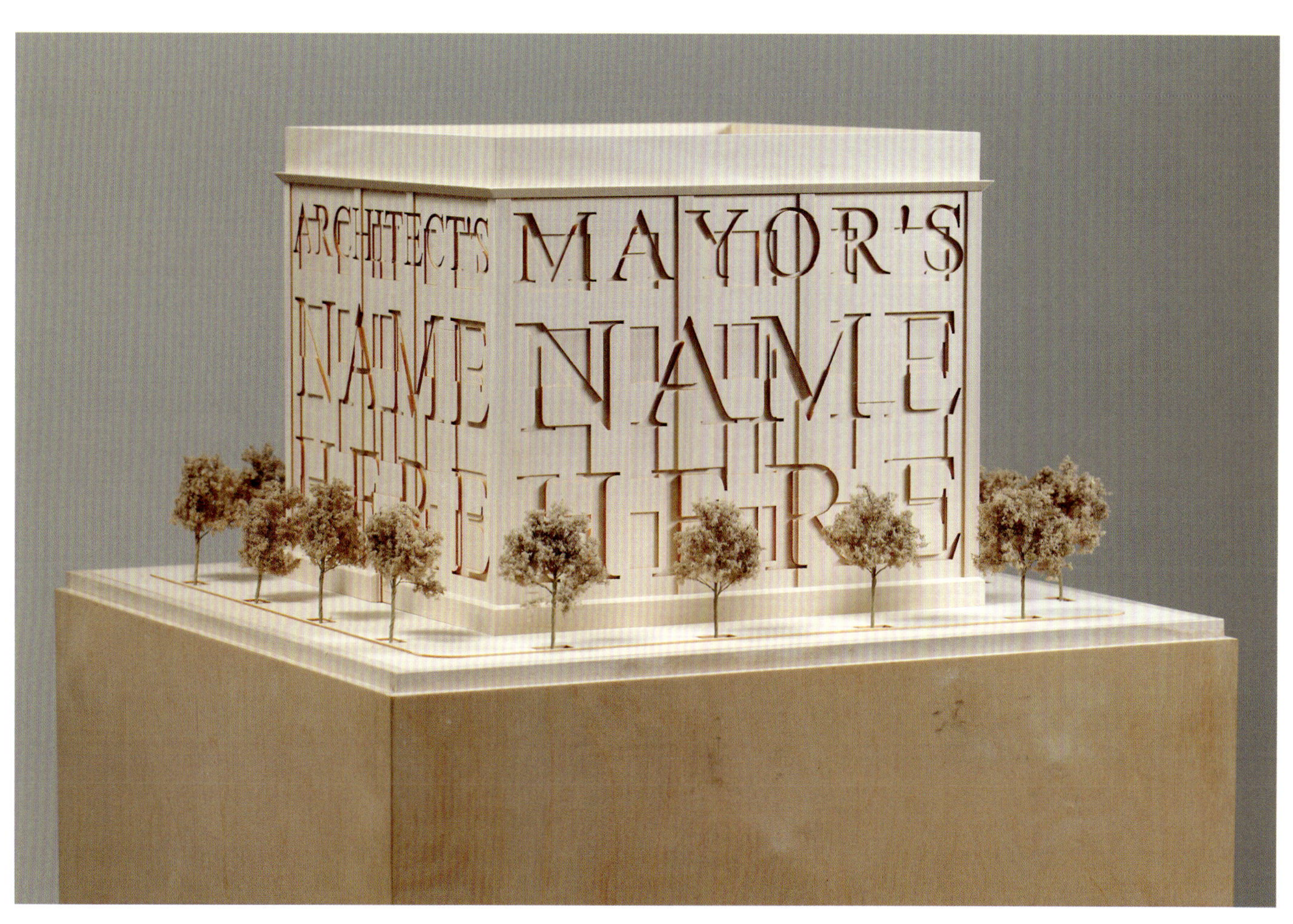
ARCHITECT'S
NAME
HERE
MAYOR'S
NAME
HERE

SOME GIFTS

2008

Cast plaster and paint

12 × 12 × 9 inches

Collection of the artist

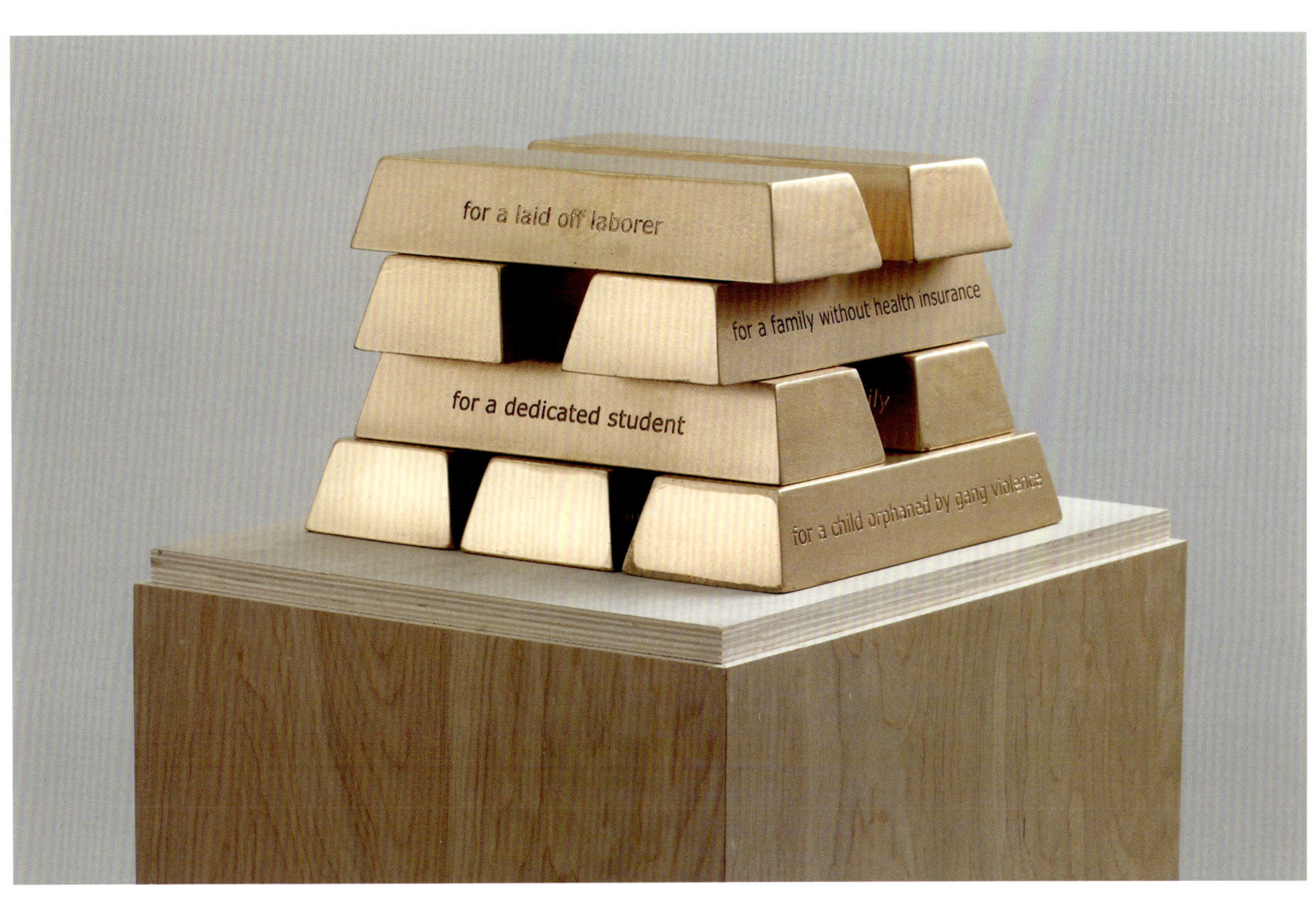
for a laid off laborer
for a family without health insurance
for a dedicated student
for a child orphaned by gang violence

NAPOLEON'S MRI

2004

Screenprint on paper

16 × 12.5 inches

Collection of Jordan D. Schnitzer

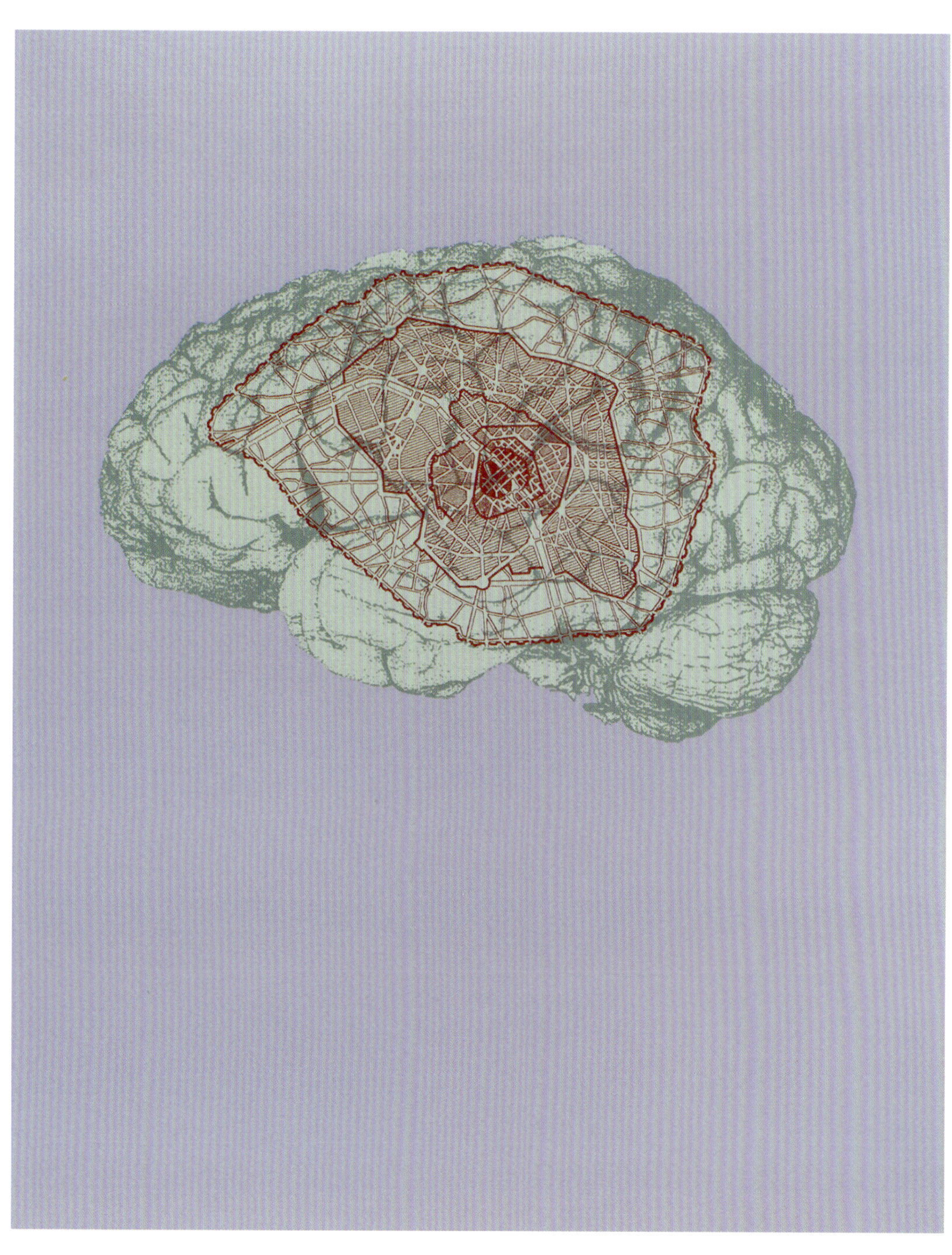

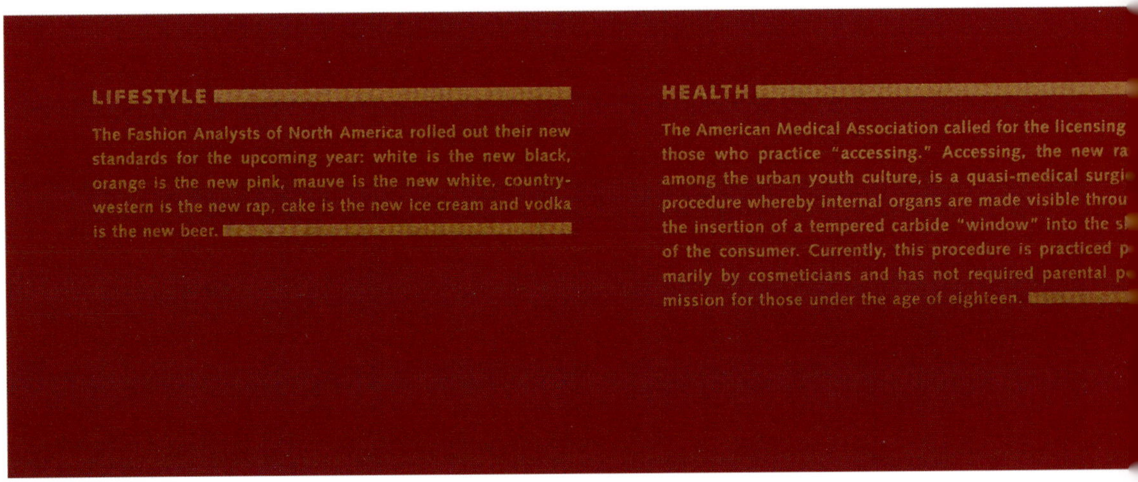

LIFESTYLE

The Fashion Analysts of North America rolled out their new standards for the upcoming year: white is the new black, orange is the new pink, mauve is the new white, country-western is the new rap, cake is the new ice cream and vodka is the new beer.

HEALTH

The American Medical Association called for the licensing
those who practice "accessing." Accessing, the new ra
among the urban youth culture, is a quasi-medical surgi
procedure whereby internal organs are made visible throu
the insertion of a tempered carbide "window" into the s
of the consumer. Currently, this procedure is practiced p
marily by cosmeticians and has not required parental p
mission for those under the age of eighteen.

NEWS FROM TOMORROW

2004

Screenprint on paper

5 × 47 inches

Collection of Jordan D. Schnitzer

oday in a formal to the allegations nes are computer ns." The statement with football offi- osoft, Dreamworks s in response to a on Friday by a dis- ng that viewers at me with different he field.

CONSUMER NEWS

Last-minute Christmas shoppers beware. In a novel approach to boost holiday sales, the National Retailers Association of America announced today that they will divide the holiday shopping season into two purchasing opportunities. The first period will stretch from October 1 to November 30 and the second from December 1 to December 26. During the December period shoppers will need to purchase a "Preferred Late Shopper Card" in order to gain access to stores. Only those holding cards will be permitted to shop during the month of December. Cards will cost $350, are only good for one holiday season, and may be obtained at any Gold Level Signature One Premier Starbucks location.

TODAY'S SCORES

San Francisco East—in overtime 5, Syracuse 78, Wyoming 284, Phoenix—cancelled due to infestation, Central City 2, Dallas—cancelled due to snow, Seattle 7.3, San Francisco West—still in litigation, Akron 32, Chicago 14, Wal-Mart 96, Thompson City 7, San Jose—team medications lost in transit—game delayed, Baghdad 8, Sony 17, Boston 42, Cleveland—cancelled due to stadium collapse, Fresno-Rosenbaum-Gonzales 70.

TIONAL

dirty bomb clean-up continues at Disneyland in Ana-
. Although Disneyland officials have said they intend to
uild the park, it is still unclear if it will be undertaken at
ark's original location.

lated news, a spokesperson for the families of the vic-
announced today that a memorial is in the planning
es with an open international design competition set to
n in December.

WEATHER

Temperatures continue.

SPORTS

The National Football League reiterate
release to the press that there is no tru
that the live action broadcast of their
enhanced for "entertainment consideratio
was delivered outside of the NFL offices
cials flanked by representatives from Mic
SKG, Pixar, CBS, and Nike. The release w
suit filed in the New York Circuit Courts
gruntled Jets season-ticket holder allegi
home were watching a more exciting g
plays than what he was paying to see o

THE LAST MOMENTS PRECEDING THE DEATH OF CIVILITY

2004

Digital print on paper

20 × 79 inches

Collection of Jordan D. Schnitzer

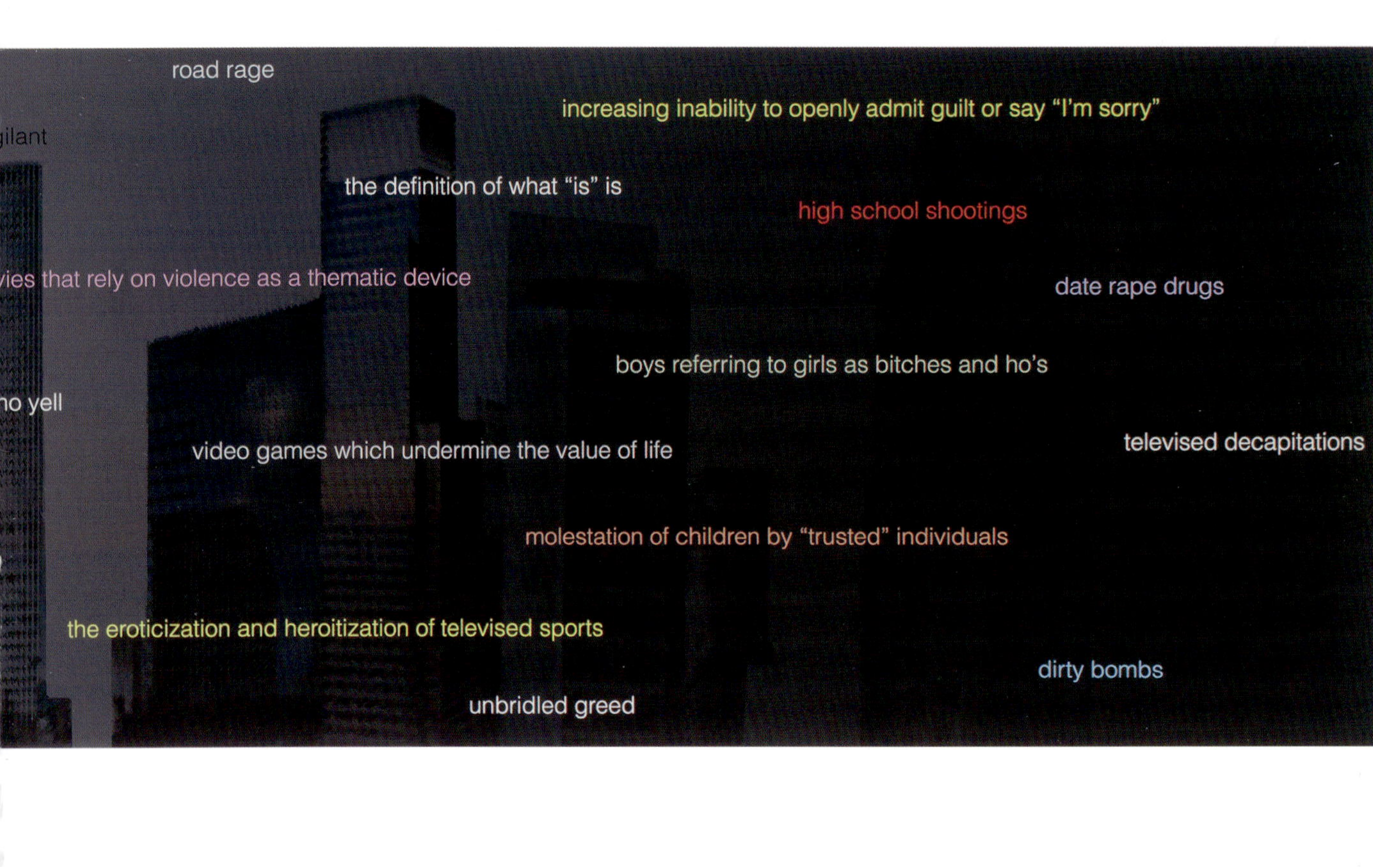

road rage
increasing inability to openly admit guilt or say "I'm sorry"
gilant
the definition of what "is" is
high school shootings
vies that rely on violence as a thematic device
date rape drugs
boys referring to girls as bitches and ho's
no yell
video games which undermine the value of life
televised decapitations
molestation of children by "trusted" individuals
the eroticization and heroitization of televised sports
dirty bombs
unbridled greed

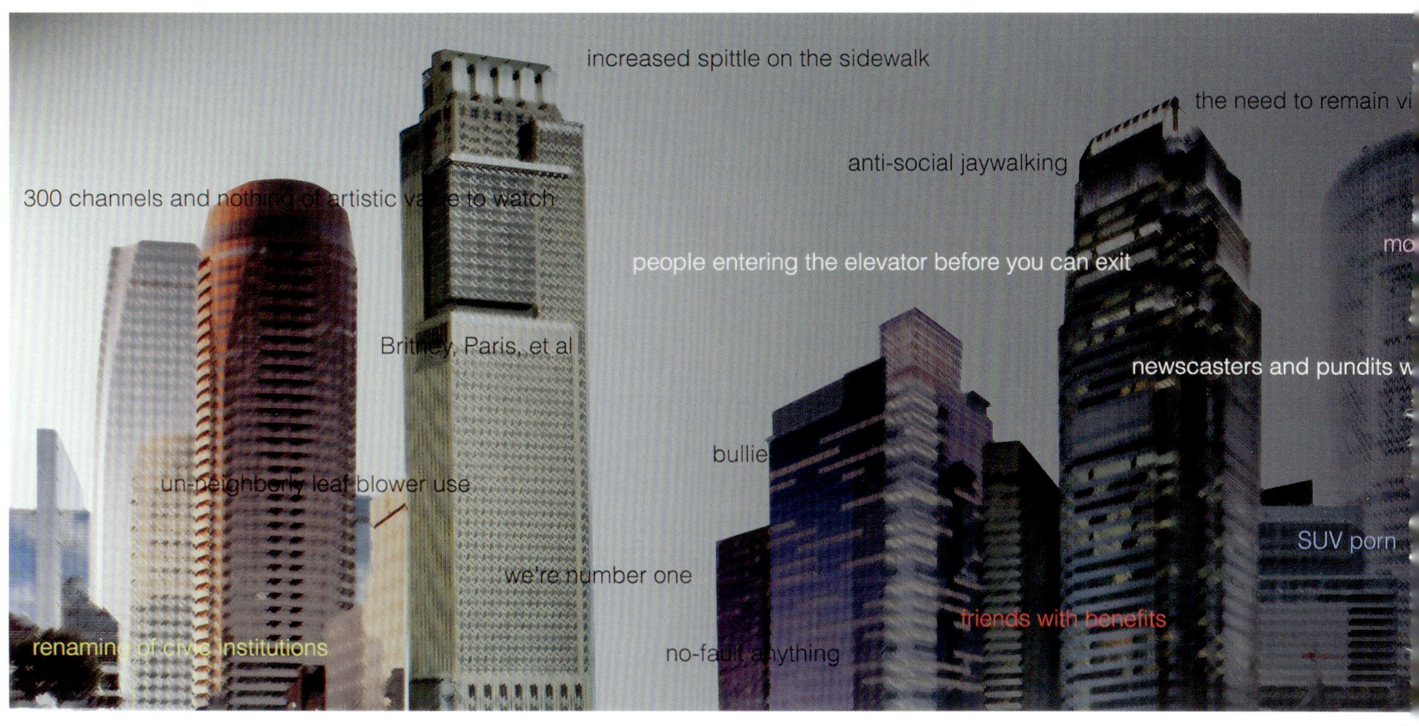

increased spittle on the sidewalk
the need to remain vi
anti-social jaywalking
300 channels and nothing of artistic value to watch
mo
people entering the elevator before you can exit
Britney, Paris, et al
newscasters and pundits w
bullie
un-neighborly leaf blower use
SUV porn
we're number one
friends with benefits
renaming of civic institutions
no-fault anything

H5N1 VIRUS CENTRAL LIBRARY DISTRIBUTION PAD

2006

Mixed media

4 × 14 × 14.5 inches

Collection of the artist

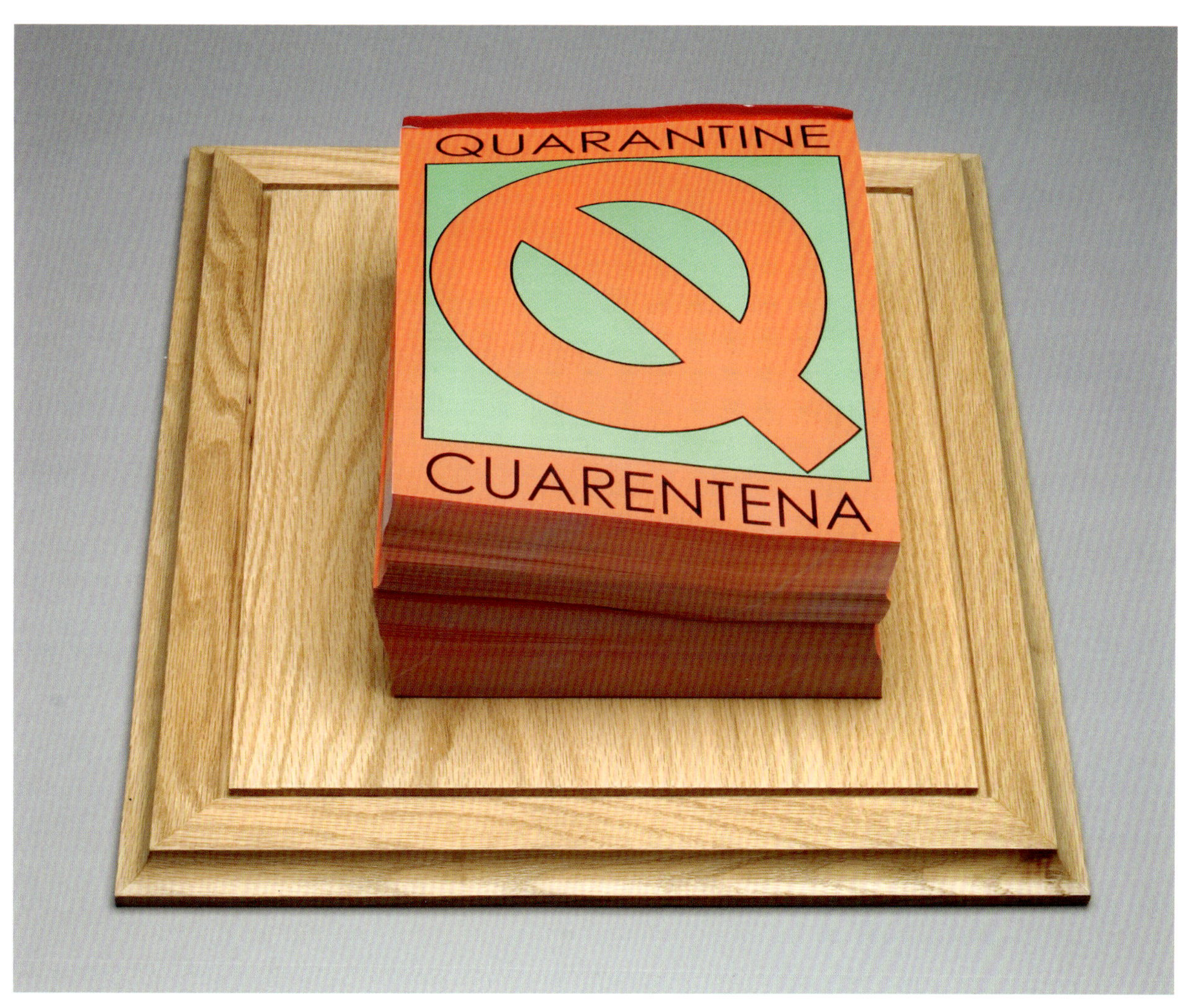
QUARANTINE
CUARENTENA

OCCURRENCES

2014

Digital print on paper

44 × 31 inches

Collection of Jordan D. Schnitzer

OCCURRENCES

1. CHILDREN, UPON REACHING THE AGE OF FIVE, SHALL BE TRANSFERRED BY THEIR PARENTS TO PRIVATE OR STATE-RUN "BOARDING KINDERGARTENS".

2. CITIZENS WILL RIOT TO PROTEST THE LACK OF BEAUTY IN GOVERNMENT-COMMISSIONED ARCHITECTURE.

3. LAWYERS WILL REQUEST, AND STANDARDIZE THE PRACTICE OF, AWARDING THEMSELVES ANNUAL BONUSES TO SUPPORT THEIR "CHOSEN QUALITY OF LIFESTYLE".

4. NEWBORN INFANTS WILL ARRIVE WITH 100% IMMUNITY TO THE EFFECTIVENESS OF ALL EXISTING ANTIBIOTICS, DUE TO FEARS OF ADVERSELY IMPACTING THE HIGHLY PROFITABLE MEDICAL TOURISM INDUSTRY, ALL FURTHER RESEARCH INTO COMBATING INFANT DISEASES WILL BE CURTAILED.

5. EXTENSIVE TRACTS OF LAND INCLUDED WITHIN NATIONAL PARK LANDS SHALL BE SOLD TO THE PRIVATE SECTOR FOR NEW DEVELOPMENT PROJECTS.

6. 40.000 PEOPLE A YEAR DIE FROM AIR POLLUTION.

1. China 2014
2. Rome 2014
3. America 2014
4. India 2014
5. America 2014
6. Paris 2005

EVERYTHING IS BROKEN

2014

Digital print on paper

51 × 38 inches

Collection of Jordan D. Schnitzer

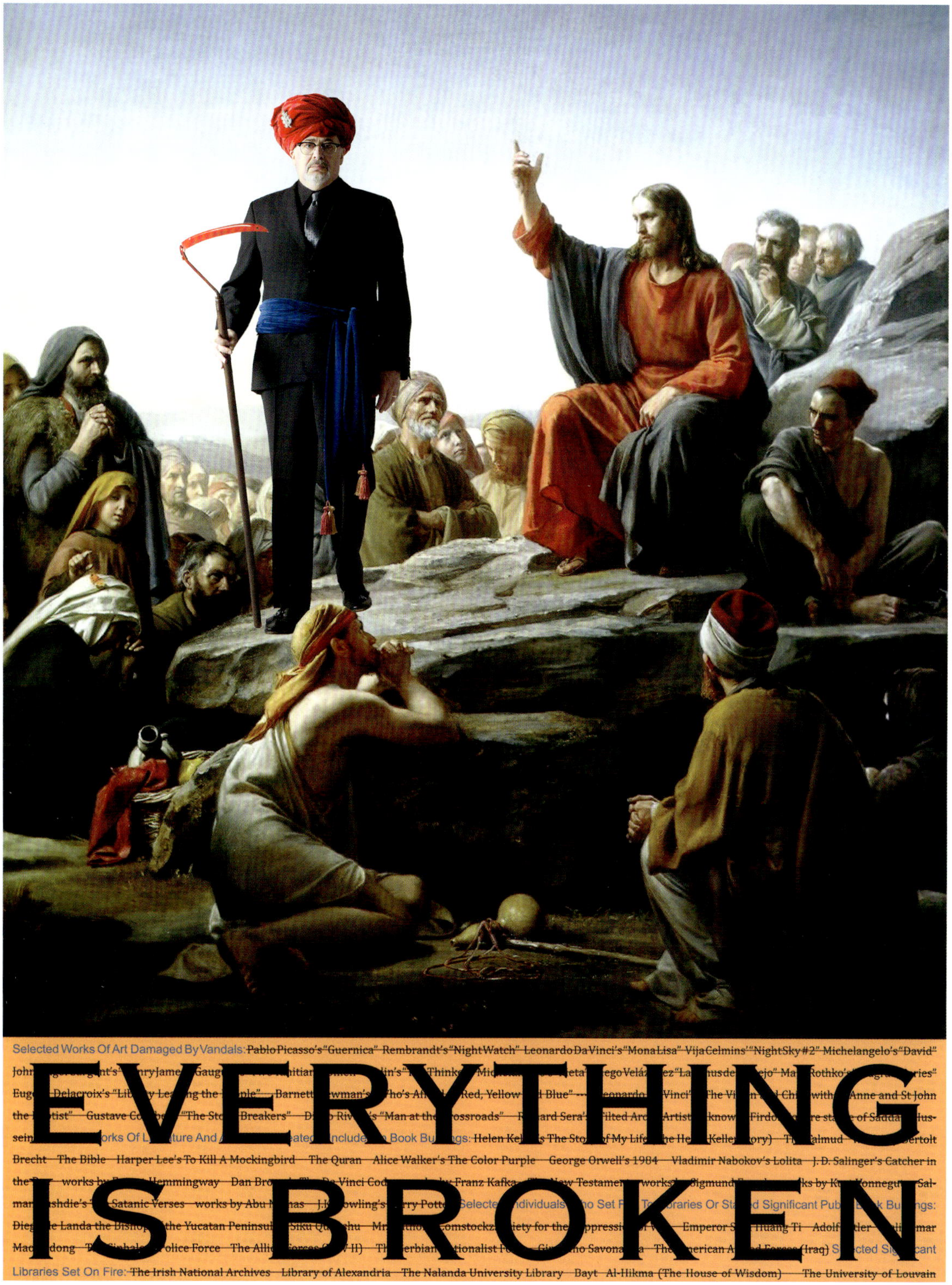

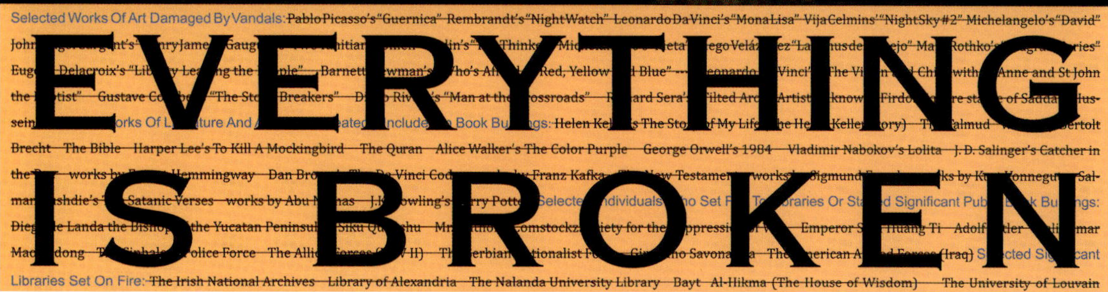

Selected Works Of Art Damaged By Vandals: Pablo Picasso's "Guernica" Rembrandt's "Night Watch" Leonardo Da Vinci's "Mona Lisa" Vija Celmins' "Night Sky #2" Michelangelo's "David"
EVERYTHING
Brecht The Bible Harper Lee's To Kill A Mockingbird The Quran Alice Walker's The Color Purple George Orwell's 1984 Vladimir Nabokov's Lolita J. D. Salinger's Catcher in
IS BROKEN
Libraries Set On Fire: The Irish National Archives Library of Alexandria The Nalanda University Library Bayt Al-Hikma (The House of Wisdom) The University of Louvain

2064: ENGLAND'S MASTER ARCHITECT PRESENTS, TO THE HOUSE OF COMMONS, THE PLAN TO ADD MINARETS TO BUCKINGHAM PALACE

2014

Digital print on paper

22 × 33 inches

Collection of Jordan D. Schnitzer

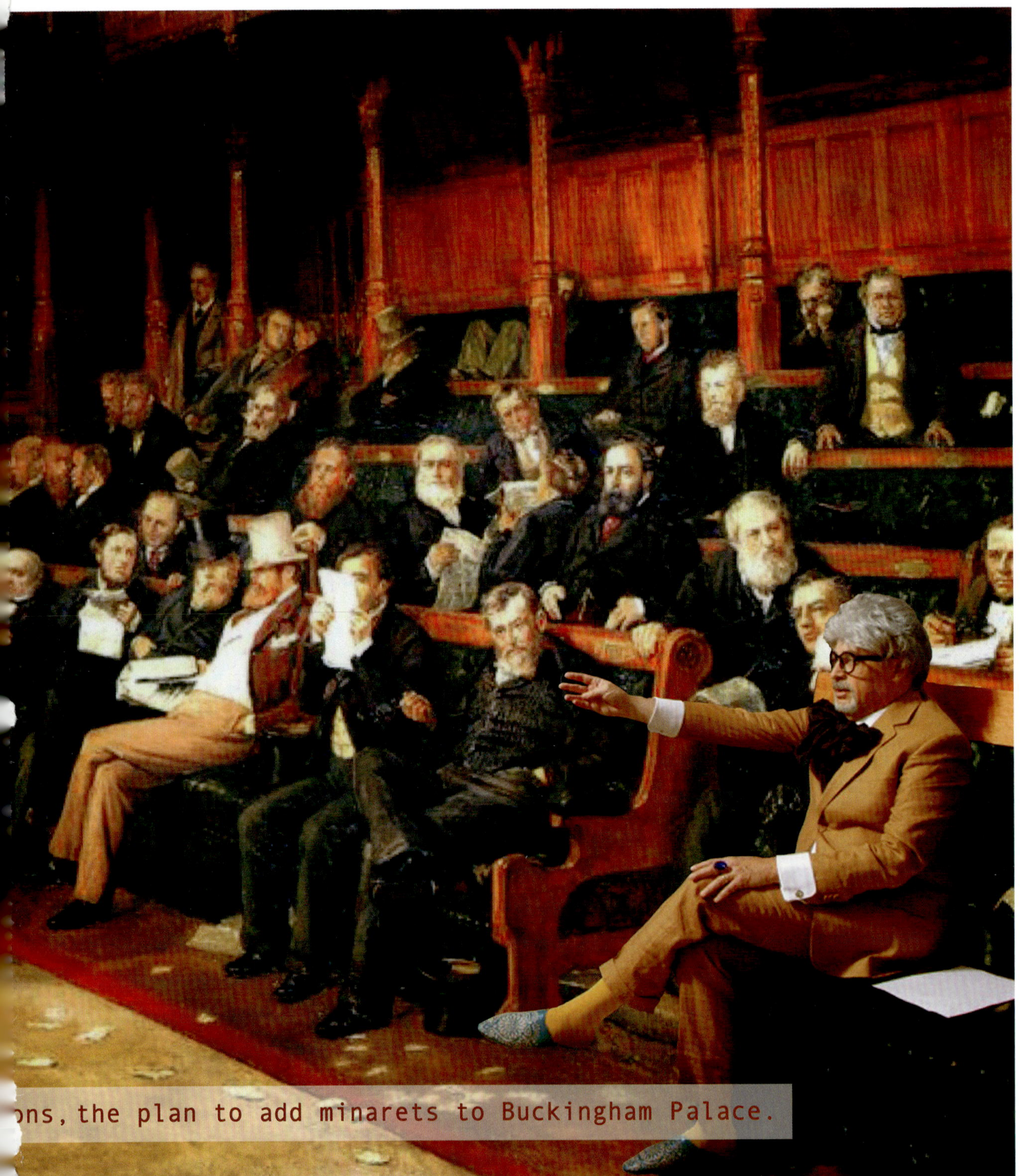

ons, the plan to add minarets to Buckingham Palace.

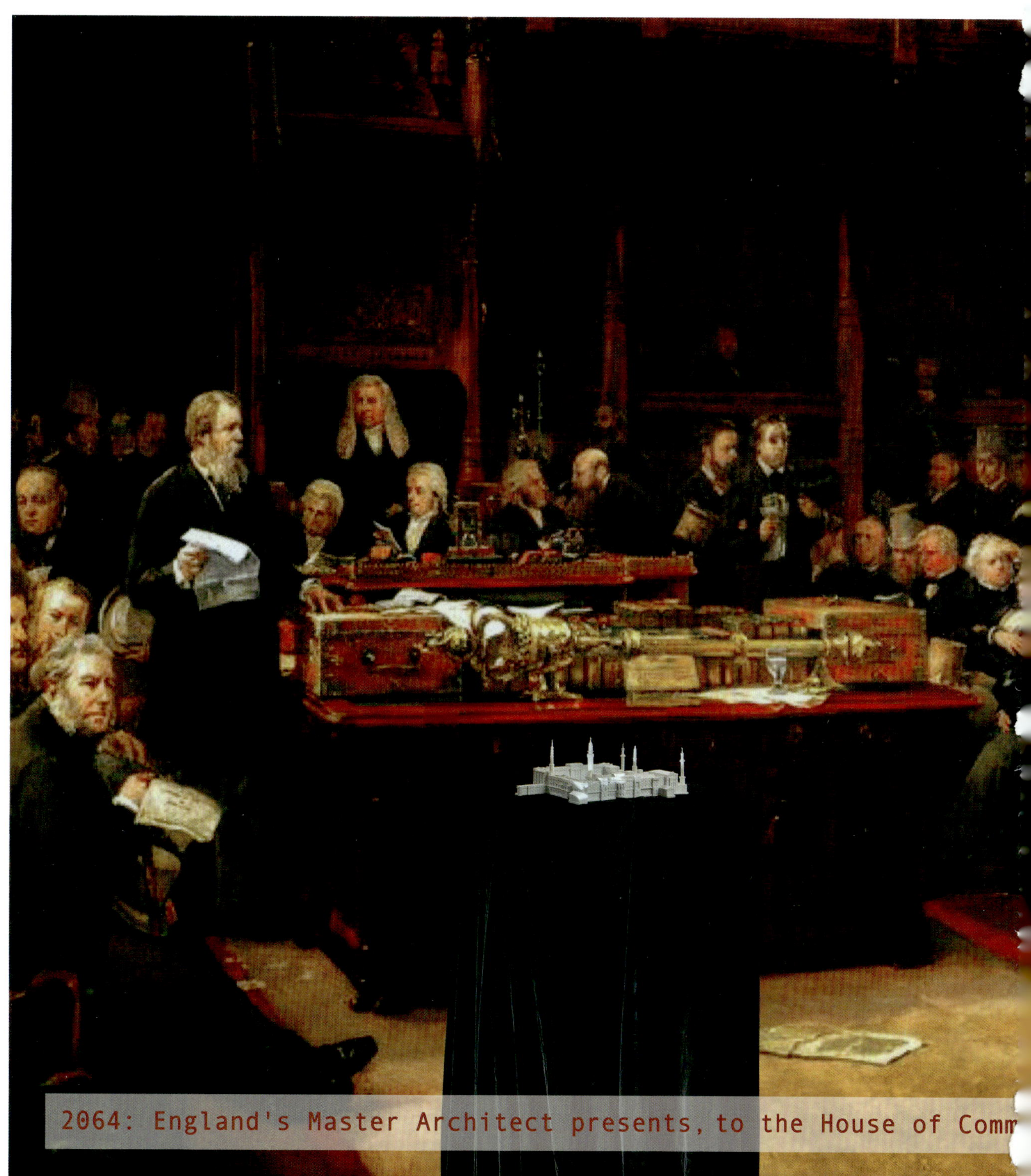
2064: England's Master Architect presents, to the House of Comm

THE NEW MAN

2014

Digital print on paper

14 × 11.5 inches

Collection of Jordan D. Schnitzer

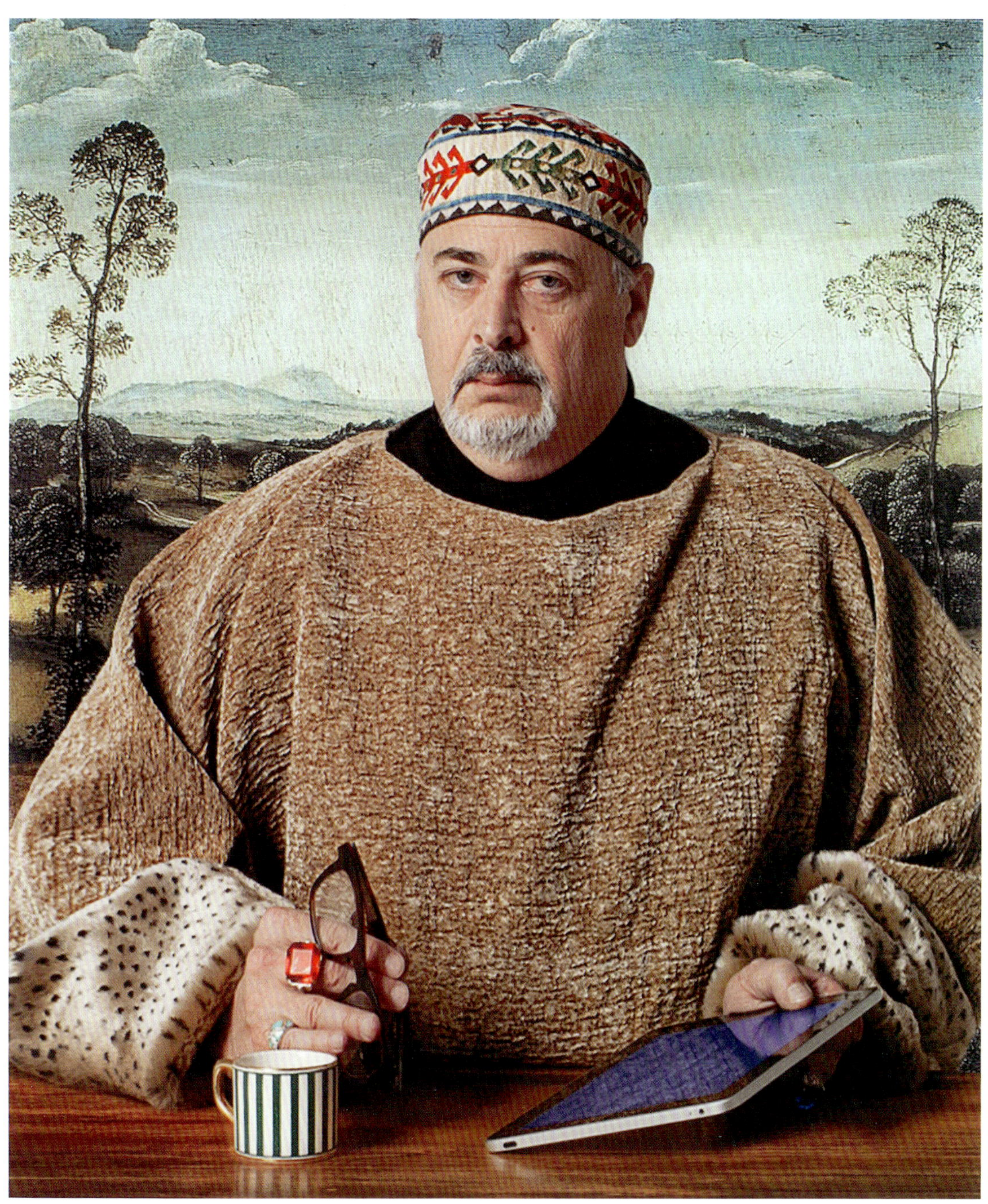

PICTURES THAT TALK

LINDA TESNER

For over four decades, the work of the artist Tad Savinar has invited the viewer to engage in conversation. The book you now hold in your hands seeks to continue that discussion. The fourteen works here have been selected to illustrate the core tenets of Savinar's work. Each piece delivers a sucker-punch to the viewer (albeit with a velvet glove), and asks the viewer to engage with the work and the artist in a dialogue about the complexities of the human experience, both sacred and profane.

Words and imagery have been frequent companions in works of art for centuries—think of the Limbourg Brothers' *Très Riches Heures du Duc du Berry* (1412–16) or cubist still lifes. But the 1980s launched a proliferation of artists who incorporate text into their work. Here we will look at Savinar's work in relationship to that of his closest contemporaries, artists who employ text as their conceptual foundation, most notably Barbara Kruger (b. 1945), Jenny Holzer (b. 1950), and Ed Ruscha (b. 1937). For Kruger, the image (usually photographic black and white) and text (usually in Futura Bold Oblique or Helvetica Ultra Condensed in red-on-white or white-on-red) is declarative: "I shop therefore I am," "Your body is a battleground," "You become what you consume." Kruger, like Savinar, is looking at cultural constructions, in particular power and gender politics. Holzer, like Kruger, is a political artist, using socially critical commentary; her early *Truisms* (1978–87) involved maxims that were widely "consumed" as photostats, T-shirts, billboards, and other formats. They were one-liners that were equally thoughtful and aggressive: "A lot of professionals are crackpots," or "Abuse of power comes as no surprise." Scale is important to Holzer. Her momentous installation *For the Guggenheim* (2008) at the Solomon R. Guggenheim Museum in New York City involved building-scale light projections of her own writings and excerpts of poetry by Wisława Szymborska onto the iconic spiral of the Frank Lloyd Wright façade.

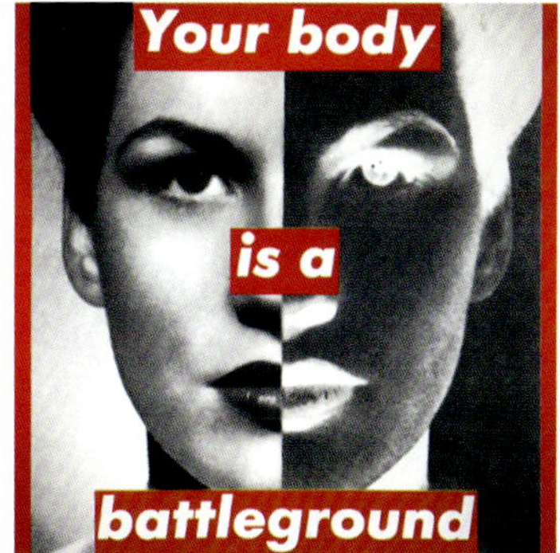

Fig. 1 Barbara Kruger, Untitled (*Your body is a battleground*), 1989. Photographic silkscreen on vinyl, 112 × 112 in. © Barbara Kruger, courtesy of the Mary Boone Gallery, New York. MBG #508.

On the surface, Kruger's and Holzer's work might remind one of some of Savinar's, but mainly because of the use of text. Everything about the use of text in the hands of Kruger and Holzer makes one feel as though the artist is shouting at the viewer—the equivalent of an e-mail message in all caps—urgent and, in some ways, intransigent in concept. Kruger and Holzer use image and graphics to get the viewer's attention. Savinar, dissimilarly, uses

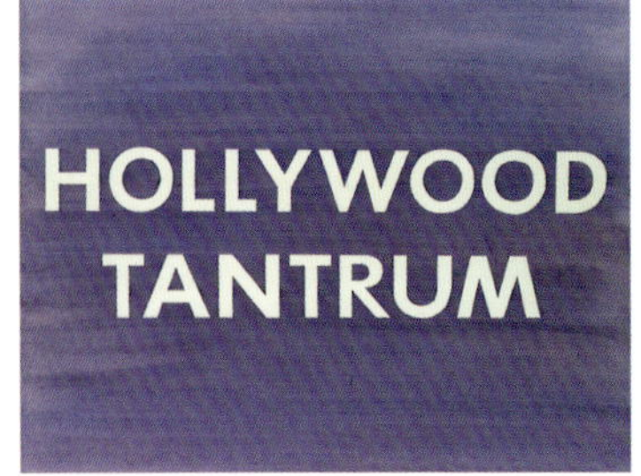

Fig. 2 Ed Ruscha, *Hollywood Tantrum*, 1979. Pastel on paper, 23 × 29 in. © Ed Ruscha. Photo: Courtesy of the Artist.

language both *as* image and *in combination with image* not to indoctrinate, shock, or rant, but to *engage in conversation*. Perhaps the difference seems subtle, but the way in which the viewer absorbs the image, and then responds to it, is at the core of Savinar's practice.

In terms of language in combination with image, the work of the Los Angeles artist Ed Ruscha somewhat parallels Savinar's and, certainly, it is the artist to whom Savinar is most often compared. And there are some important similarities. Ruscha, like Savinar, is a master of language as semiotics. He also invents statements—sometimes exegetic, as in *I Don't Want No Retro Spective* (1979), sometimes purely invented through an intuitive sense of word combinations, as in *God Knows Where* (2014). Ruscha's work is closely related to the mythology of the West, Southern California in particular. "California was a real lift for me," Ruscha has claimed, "It was swanky and slick, its drive-in and drive-by architecture, perfect weather, palm trees, beaches and waves—it promised a faster life than I had known."[1] So much about Ruscha's choices, of imagery and language, invokes nostalgia (gas stations, parking lots, swimming pools) or the romance of a broad horizon, as if one is viewing a Ruscha painting through the windshield of a car or on the expanse of a movie screen. Savinar, too, seduces his viewer with wistfulness and romance, but his use of those beguiling stylistic elements is never meant to be sexy or cool.

There is another important difference between Ruscha and Savinar. Ruscha relishes the objectness of his work; he has made books that he considers sculptural art objects, and, for a few years, he even painted on the sides of his canvases to accentuate the idea that a painting is a three-dimensional object.[2] Savinar, on the other hand, always underscores the primacy of his artwork as *image*, a distinction that will be discussed shortly.

Perhaps the artist whose work resonates most closely with Savinar's is the American artist and writer Joe Brainard (1942–1994).[3] Many art historians suggest that Brainard's work shares an affinity with pop (his "Nancy" drawings), but Brainard's work does not fit the genre. Andy Warhol and Roy Lichtenstein maintained an ironic distance from their subject matter; Brainard actually showed fondness and amusement for his subjects, using his observations of the world to beguile his viewer/reader and elicit a feeling of comradery and complicity. Brainard made artists' books, such as *29 Mini-Essays* (1978), in which he posits odd aphorisms: "History: What with history piling up so fast, almost every day is the anniversary of something awful," or "Pride: Pride creates its own banana peels." Brainard is perhaps best known for his book *I Remember* (1975), a lexicon expanding into 138 pages of simple, nostalgic sentiments: "I remember after people are gone thinking of things I should have said but didn't"[4] or "I remember peach colored evenings just before dark,"[5] or "I remember 'hard' Christmas candy. Especially the ones with flower designs. I remember not liking the ones with jelly in the middle very much."[6] And in a later conceptual book, *Ten Imaginary Still Lifes* (1991), ten short paragraphs describe the components of a still life but without any illustration; the composition can only be completed in the reader's imagination. "I close my eyes. I see a white statue (say 10″ high) of David . . . this still life is secretly smiling."[7]

Savinar has created a number of art books, ephemera, and sculptural works that share a stylistic aesthetic with Brainard's work. Viewers will notice a similarity between Savinar's attention to the way text reads and Brainard's straightforward classic fonts and minimal graphics. Savinar's *Courtesy Card* (2006) lists a number of things that citizens could or should do to be more considerate of fellow city dwellers: "Turn your music down a little"; "Get control of your dog/child/spouse/partner/other"; "Re-examine the placement of your vehicle in relation to the space allotted." The "friendly suggestions" were printed on three-by-five-inch cards with a little tick box next to each request, so that presumably one could carry around a supply of cards, check the appropriate box when one witnessed an infraction, and graciously impart some constructive criticism to the perpetrator. A similar work, Savinar's *7 Reasons to Be Optimistic* (2006), is a series of seven wall-mounted statements that are etched into glass: "I saw a young couple kissing while they waited for their bus to arrive" and "I almost rear-ended a pickup when it stopped suddenly to let a squirrel run across the street." It is hard to know if Brainard was as obsessive about the "look" of his writings—probably not, because they were produced by a publisher—but Savinar is exceedingly exact about every aspect of his image; text, font, and spacing are as carefully considered as content. In Savinar's work, the way the text *looks*—slightly didactic and easy-to-read—is

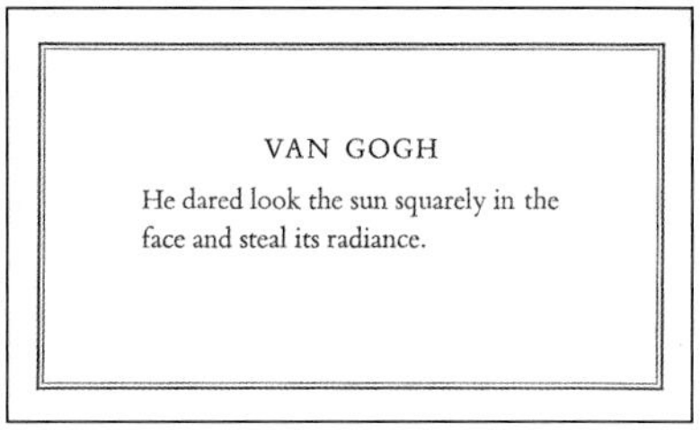

VAN GOGH

He dared look the sun squarely in the face and steal its radiance.

Fig. 3 Joe Brainard, "Van Gogh," from *29 Mini-Essays*, from *The Collected Writings of Joe Brainard*, edited by Ron Padgett (New York: Library of America, 2012).

extremely important. Savinar wants the look of his text to feel familiar to his viewer, to persuade the viewer into reading the text and thereby absorbing the context. Both Brainard and Savinar trade on the hope that they will engage their viewer/reader into an authentic dialogue.[8]

It is hard to find an artist working today whose work is as complex and multi-layered as that of Tad Savinar. Simultaneously, it is the complexity of human life that stokes Savinar's studio practice. He is an assiduous observer of our contemporary world—the beauty and wonder of it all, yes, but also the conundrums, paradoxes, injustices, ironies, and horrors. His work is a little like a mirror held up to the viewer so that he/she might become cognizant of some aspect of the world we share *as well as* see himself/herself in it. But Savinar is a careful and thoughtful communicator; he is not strictly interested in dogma or advocacy, except insofar as his ideas *engage* the viewer in a conceptual conversation. It is as if in each of his works, Savinar is asking the viewer: "Sometimes I feel like this; I wonder if you do, too?"

Savinar launched his studio practice in 1973, a decade when performance and conceptual art reigned, but when emerging artists were still inculcated with the idea that "the artist makes the art." John Baldessari's 1971 video *I Am Making Art*, in which he stands before a blank wall making simple arm gestures and repeating, "I am making art," is iconic for establishing the perception that art need not be a slave to a finished object. But—and this is significant—the primacy of Baldessari as "the artist," making the gestures (and therefore the art) himself, is undeniable. He didn't hire an actor and shoot against a green screen.

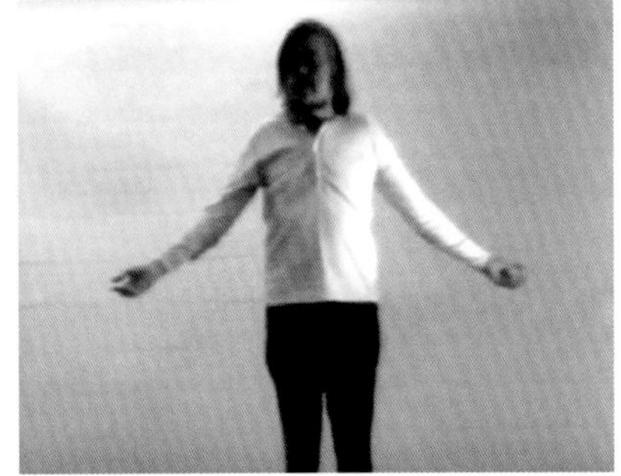

Fig. 4 John Baldessari, film still from *I Am Making Art*, 1971. Black-and-white video, 15 minutes. © John Baldessari. Photo: Courtesy of the Artist.

Savinar's earliest works were made of found objects or cardboard. Sometimes he experimented with the state of his own persona, photographing himself within these constructions, assuming different characters by changing his hair and clothing. In one work, *Coffin Man*, he mourned his own death by kneeling and crying over an arrow-ridden cardboard coffin. Early installations and single-artist exhibitions followed in the 1980s at venues such as Artists Space (New York), Los Angeles Institute of Contemporary Art, Portland Art Museum (Oregon), Center on Contemporary Art (Seattle), The Art Gym at

Marylhurst University (Portland), and Reed College (Portland). These exhibitions examined issues surrounding culture, family, and gender.

In the 1980s a sea change occurred in Savinar's studio practice that would demarcate an entirely new way in his art-making process. In 1983 he mounted an exhibition at The Art Gym at Marylhurst University called *Talk Radio*. He had been listening to local talk shows and noticing topics that preoccupied the callers: war, America, the media, violence, sex, religion, missing children. During the same year, Savinar curated an exhibition at the Portland Center for the Visual Arts (PCVA) in which he included work by the performance artist Eric Bogosian. Savinar conceived, then the two of them proceeded to develop, a performance work called *Talk Radio*, in which Bogosian played an acerbic talk show host.[9] It is important to note that the 1980s was the decade of the Pictures Generation. Performance and spectacle were being explored successfully by Robert Longo, Laurie Anderson, Bogosian, and Karen Finley. "Persona" photographs by Cindy Sherman, appropriation by Richard Prince and Louise Lawler, and, as previously mentioned, image/text combinations by Kruger and Holzer were defining trends of this decade. Savinar had already been experimenting with these methodologies in the '70s, using his own image in environments. This was a time, too, when Savinar was spending much of his time in New York, immersed in the national art scene.[10] *Talk Radio* ultimately went on to become an Off-Broadway stage play in 1987 and then a feature film directed by Oliver Stone in 1988.

Through his experience with *Talk Radio*, Savinar recognized the power of theater to communicate directly with the audience, an important goal that he had been seeking in his visual art practice. He went on to work exclusively writing stage plays and, for a period of about four years, from 1986 to 1990, he concentrated solely on theater.[11] He literally stopped making visual art—he gave up his studio and canceled his subscription to *Artforum*. Not only did theater provide Savinar with a format more conducive to fully exploring themes *with language* than he was formerly able to do in visual art but he also discovered that the process of theater production—an arena where many individuals' skills are deployed to support the final production—was diametrically opposed to his experience as a visual artist—working primarily alone and making each

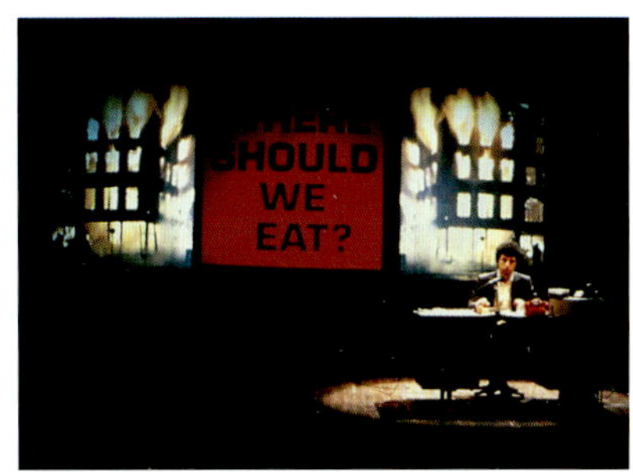

Fig. 5 *Talk Radio*, 1985. Eric Bogosian in performance at Portland Center for the Visual Arts; rear projection by Tad Savinar.

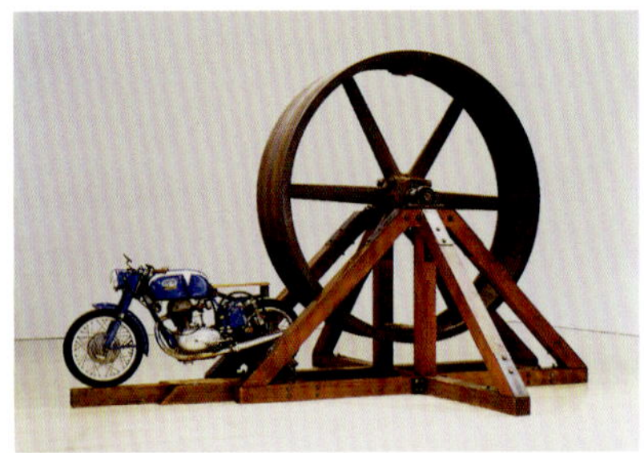

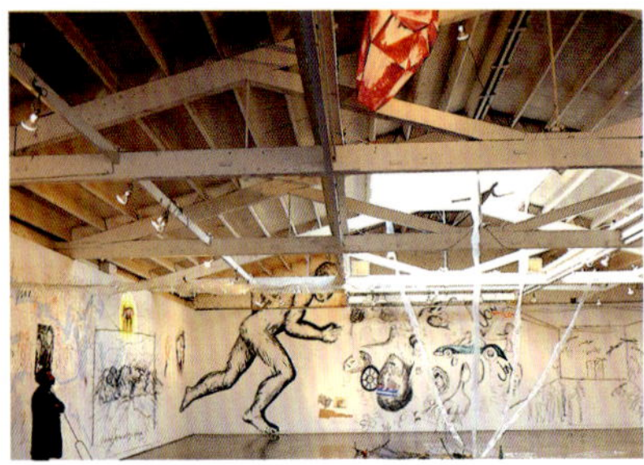

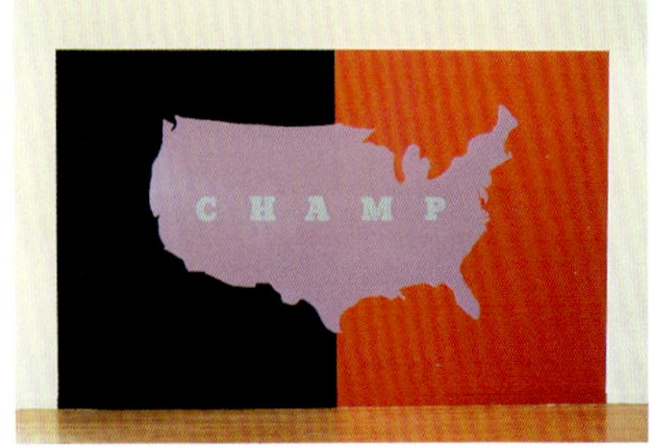

Fig. 6 Chris Burden, *The Big Wheel*, 1979. Three-ton, 8 ft. diam., cast-iron flywheel powered by a 1968 Benelli 250cc motorcycle; 112 × 175 × 143 in. © Chris Burden; image courtesy of The Burden/Rubens Revocable Trust and Gagosian Gallery.

Fig. 7 Jonathan Borofsky, *All Is One*, installation (detail), 1979. Portland Center for the Visual Arts, Portland, Oregon. © Jonathan Borofsky.

Fig. 8 Tad Savinar, *Champ*, 1983. Latex paint on wall. Photo: Wayne Aldridge.

component of a work of art himself. In theater, no one individual carries the entire production; the playwright, director, actors, set designers, stagehands, and so on each contributes specialized skills. An alternative methodology became apparent to Savinar; he could hire highly skilled craftspeople to manifest his ideas exactly as he envisioned them in his studio practice, working processes also used by Robert Longo, Chris Burden, Jeff Koons, and many other artists at this time. He could hire a specialist—a sign painter, an architectural model maker, a printmaker, a photographer, a foundry—to construct work based on his very detailed ideas and specifications.[12] From the 1990s forward, he acquired a certain freedom to deeply explore concepts and manifest his ideas deliberately, which made it possible for him to resume his studio practice in 1990.

All of Savinar's work is content driven. Content, and the coequal need to engage the viewer, is paramount to him. Once he has settled on a condition worthy of exploration, he is challenged to determine the best way to deliver the message. His ideas coalesce in a wide variety of mediums—he is just as apt to make a sculpture as a print, a painting, a drawing, or a book.

Savinar is an obsessive list-maker, but one wonders: How does he first develop a master list of potential texts to be used for a particular project, then whittle and edit the list until it is *exactly* the language he wants to commit to a work of art? He says that the exercise usually starts with some sort of observation about contemporary culture.

Savinar is fond of saying of his prints, "It's an *image*, not an *object*." In the 1980s he painted directly on gallery walls. This grew out of his desire to eliminate the "wonder" of the object, an aim also achieved during the early '80s by Mike Glier's and Jonathan Borofsky's wall paintings. Savinar's thinking was that if he removed all physicality, skill, and execution, the image itself would propel the viewer into a conversation about content. This subtle but important distinction is noticed in the way Savinar presents his works. He always takes care to mat the image of the prints, instead of floating them in a frame. In this way, he underscores the idea that the print is about the image represented, not the preciousness or "sacred objectness" of the print on paper. He does not worship

IN PURSUIT OF JOY (detail)

the page, nor does he want his work to be conspicuous in any way: the physical artwork is only the delivery system for information.

Savinar does not shy away from using beauty to draw his viewer into content. *In Pursuit of Joy* (1998) evolved out of a simple query posed to him: What brings you joy? The question motivated Savinar to start with his signature list, and then decide how he wanted to present it. In this case, he wanted something to underscore the idea of joy—fabric, perhaps, instead of quotidian paper. And toile, because its romantic, bucolic design tugs at one's memories of comfort and home.

The text in *In Pursuit of Joy* is screenprinted onto blue-and-white toile, emblematic of tasteful American middle-class decorating. The imagery on the textile is a traditional pastoral idyll—one boy with a goat, another with a butterfly net, lovers idling under a tree, country musicians, and figures strolling near a stream. In fact, the material is the same fabric that covered the couch in the living room of the home in which Savinar grew up. For the text, he asked his father to write out the list in his handwriting, which Savinar then appropriated for the piece. Here there are literally layers of visual and conceptual nostalgia that reflect on family of origin issues, how they shape us, and how humans tend to transmute memory into core values. The irony in this work, and in many other Savinar pieces, provides a subtle comic relief, a softened edge to the gravitas of Savinar's concepts.

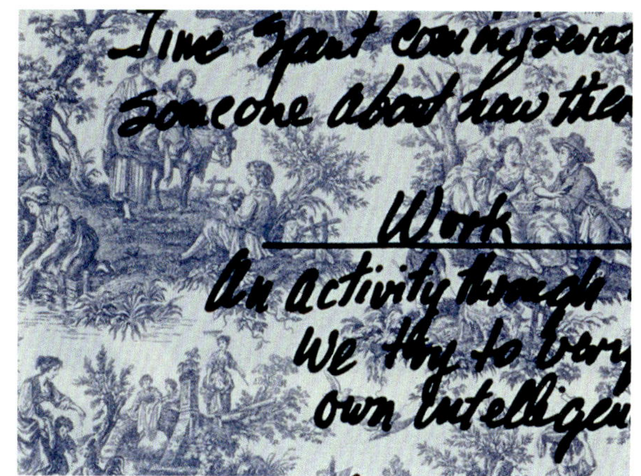

In Pursuit of Joy lists major categories through which humans presumably experience joy: "Friendship," "Work," "Marriage," "Children," "Community Service," and "Being Alone." These states of being might, more realistically, reflect circumstances in which people experience satisfaction, or gratification—the suggestion, in the title, that these factors elicit absolute happiness is typical of Savinar's careful use of language. Here, "joy" seems hyperbolic and cheeky—yes, one might find moments of joy in friendship, or marriage, but it is a comment on contemporary societal values that anyone would expect such consistent heights in any of these categories. How much more realistic would it be to title this work "In Pursuit of Contentment?" or

WONDERS OF HEREDITY (detail)

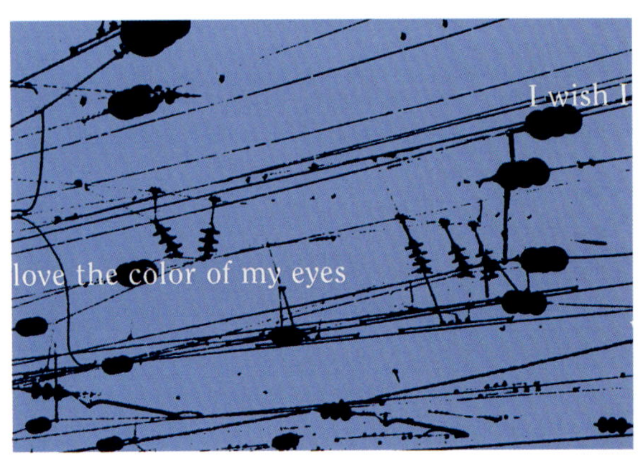

"In Pursuit of Complacency?" Savinar's caustic tone is further revealed under "Community Service," altruistically defined as "The attempt to make things better for the next guy (who we all know could care less)"—but "Children, An investment in the future" is a more hopeful sentiment.

Wonders of Heredity (2001) is another screenprint, here on paper, that presents five statements that probe at sentiments about the speaker's genetic heritage and establish some familial characteristics:

> everyone in our family is a good swimmer
>
> I wish I had an ear for music
>
> I love the color of my eyes
>
> I wish I was a twin
>
> why can't I dance like my brother

The text overlays a slightly dissolved image of telephone poles with wires that rope across the field of blue paper, punctuated by fuses, transformers, and insulators. This is a skyward view one would find near a train yard. Metaphorically, the crisscrossing of telephone wires suggests people "connecting" with each other, "crossing wires" and "keeping lines of communication open"—all of the complexities associated with family dynamics. The rhetorical statements pose rather superficial genetic qualities—eye color, musical ability, athleticism—but there is no hint at deeper, psychological qualities—a tendency toward being easygoing or kind, or a proclivity toward anger.

Savinar is a self-proclaimed image-collector. When asked about the telephone line imagery, he shrugs it off as an illustration from a vast store of images that he has hunted down throughout his career; it was something he had hung onto for probably ten years or more. He used to regularly peruse the Multnomah County Library's image archives and, more recently, the Internet. He is constantly looking for images that will resonate with the viewer, emotional triggers that will support his texts. He banks on his ability to collect images through his own visceral and aesthetic responses that will pique the interest of his viewers, too. Frequently, the allure of the image is the first thing that the viewer responds to, before he/she connects with the text.

Parents' Dreams (1998) is a sculptural "diptych" consisting of silk nightclothes, pajamas for a man and a nightgown for a woman. For parents-to-be, the moment of conception—symbolized for Savinar by pajamas—marks the dawning of ideas about child rearing. These luxurious night clothes, silky and silvery, are "all dressed up" for the genesis of parenting, a life change that is, by realistic accounts, anything but glamorous.

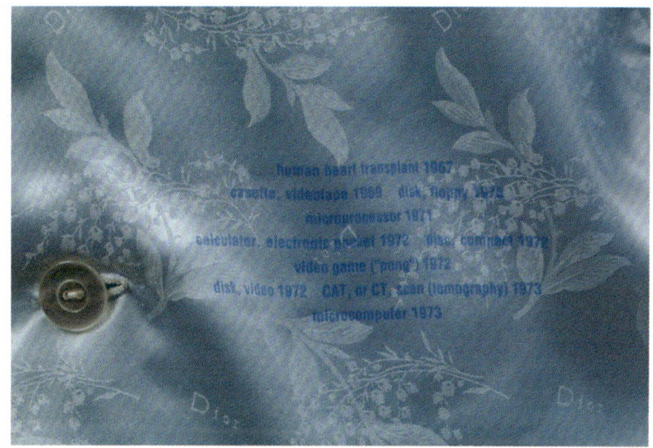

PARENTS' DREAMS (detail)

The textile used in *Parents' Dreams* is actually a "pursued object" (as opposed to a "found object"). Once Savinar decided on the idea of making pajamas, he then considered: What *kind* of pajamas? Probably not flannel, probably not seersucker; did silk correlate best with his ideas for this work? Savinar ultimately located the brocaded silk at a fabric store, and then he had the lists screenprinted onto the flat yardage at a sign shop. There is plenty of commentary in the material alone, but before the fabric was sewn into pajamas, Savinar added lists of notable milestones in technology or scientific discovery, along with the dates of their achievement. The pajamas are overlaid with the weight of human history, grouped into encapsulated periods of time.

A close look at the fabric reveals that the silk is brand-named "Dior," and the design brocaded into the material is of lilies-of-the-valley. There is intrinsic symbolism here; the lily of the valley is heavily laden with iconography. The blossom traditionally signifies purity and innocence; in some countries, it is the traditional blossom to offer at the birth of a new baby.[13] In France, May Day is celebrated by giving little bouquets of this flower; the first of May is an international holiday honoring the working class, and parenting, while potentially a source of joy and satisfaction, is also hard work.

It is engrossing to read and ponder these lists—they captivate the attentive viewer. Some facts seem slightly irrelevant, in a Trivial Pursuit sort of way. Do viewers today even know what a "slide rule" (1620) is? Or a "spinning

PARENTS' DREAMS (details)

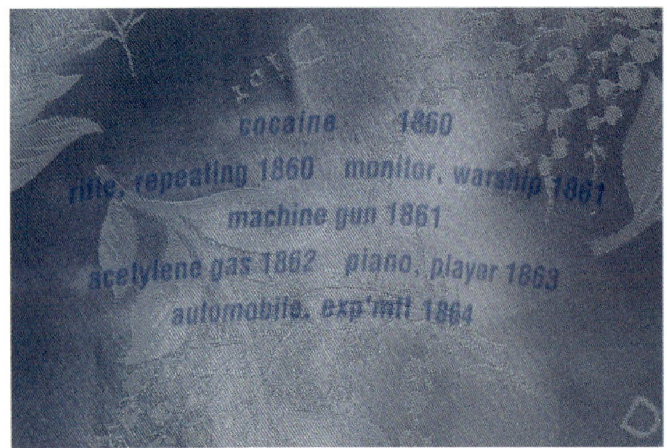

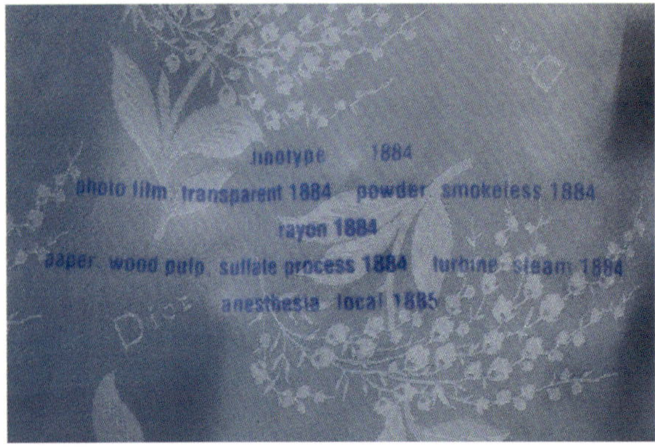

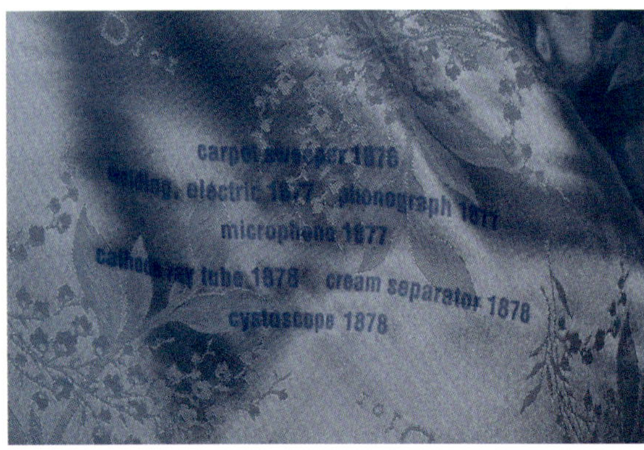

mule" (1779)? Or a "carpet sweeper" (1876)?" How about that cocaine was "discovered" in 1860? The tension between the innocent but intense self-focus symptomatic of new parenthood and the mind-boggling march through historic milestones—the micro against the macro—causes one to question one's significance against the progression of human achievement. The poignancy is figuratively pregnant with interpretation.

Patterns (2001) is a screenprinted image on paper, and it is a large print—more than five feet across, about the scale of a pull-down map that one would have found in a grade school classroom. Here Savinar explores issues parallel to those in *Parents' Dreams*. *Patterns* is both romantic and sentimental, an examination of one's hopes for one's family and a realization of the life one has lived.

The image is of an isometric map of an early frontier town. One might think that this is an early rendering of Portland—in the upper left-hand corner there is a bridge over a river, and the core settlements seem to describe early Portland platting. But the map is not identified, and that distinction is important, as the image and language are no more referential to Savinar than to the "every viewer" who experiences this work. The town conjures notions of the American frontier and all of the hopes and dreams that Westward expansion traditionally represents.

Overlaid onto the print are the following sentiments:

I learned a skill
I planted roses
I yearned for the wide open country
I appreciated a full youth
I raised a family
I anticipated the seasons

PATTERNS (detail)

Sometimes Savinar the artist is also Savinar the evaluator, looking back and taking stock of "how we are doing." The subject in *Patterns*—the "speaker" (not the image)—is caught in a life review, wondering if life choices were well made. Savinar calls this method of list-making "a fully narrative writing exercise," aimed at capturing a sentiment or sensation that his viewer might share.

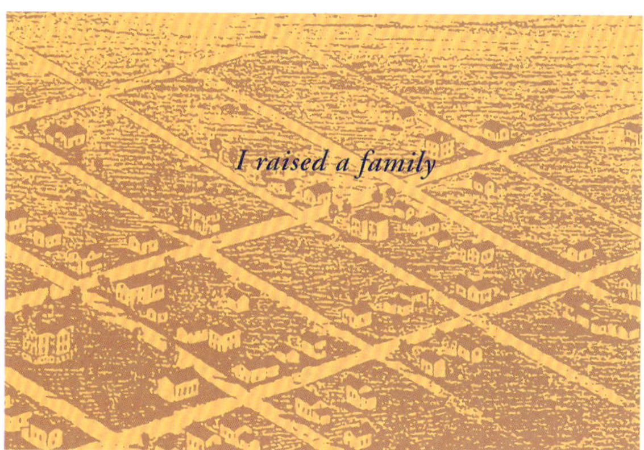

Here the text is overt self-proclamation; each statement begins with the pronoun "I." In presenting an image from a past century and combining it with voices reflective of lives lived, Savinar is asking viewers, in the *present tense*, to compare their lives to date and think about how they might reflect on their lives lived at a future moment. Again, Savinar taps into his experience as a playwright and thinks about "character" development; only in this instance the reader/viewer is being "directed" to affirm each statement, in his/her own internal voice.

In the assessment of one's life, can one's accomplishments be reduced to six bullet points? Is the achievement of "raising a family" commensurate with being sufficiently in touch with the cycles of nature so as to appreciate, say, the colors of autumn? What *are* the measures of a life well lived?

Much of Savinar's work deals with issues pertinent to community, a theme closely related to his considerations about family. He is deeply engaged by this topic, as his work in urban design and civic memorials[14] evidences. Savinar also concedes that the intimate scale of the city of Portland, defined by smaller two-hundred-by-two-hundred-foot blocks in the downtown and celebrated for its walkability, clearly plays a role in his sensitivity to what Savinar calls "the development of a shared civic and social intimacy."

Development (2006) is a sculpture that jabs at those empowered to affect the urban landscape. The piece is a traditional architectural model rendered in basswood. The building is presented on a pedestal, encircled by code-required

DEVELOPMENT (detail)

SOME GIFTS

street trees, but in addition to the placement of windows and doors, into each façade of the building is carved one of the following:

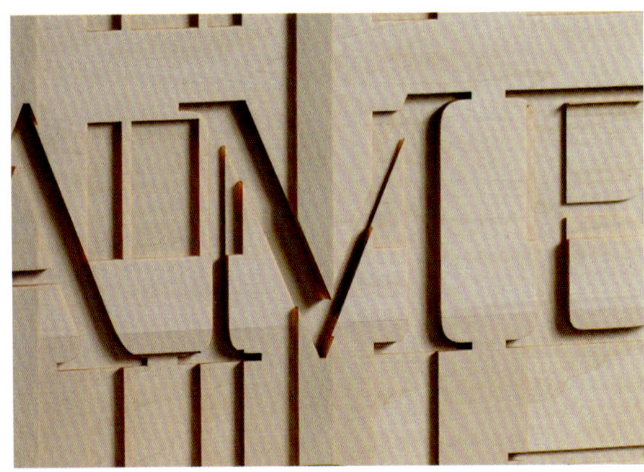

Architect's Name Here

Mayor's Name Here

Developer's Name Here

Architect's Name Here Also

Development is a visual parody closely related to Savinar's play *Cover Shot* (1989). The play anticipated a cultural trend of celebrity architects designing aggrandized and overblown museum structures.[15] Frank Lloyd Wright's Solomon R. Guggenheim Museum in New York is a classic example of a building that is a work of art in its own right, but so are Peter Eisenman's Wexner Center for the Arts in Columbus, Ohio, or Frank Gehry's Guggenheim Bilbao. The overt criticism of a standard development practice is priceless as well.[16] The piece over-exaggerates a very real paradox inherent in civic expansion. Too regularly a community landmark—a museum, an arena, a stadium, a hospital, a park—becomes an opportunity for ego-driven design foisted upon the public.

Some Gifts (2008) is a somewhat less cynical, more poignant observation of what it means to be involved in community. Here Savinar has created a simulacrum of a stack of nine gold ingots—a symbol of the basis of world economy. On the faces of the bars are phrases identifying recipients for whom the "gift" of the title is intended: "for a child orphaned by gang violence," "for an elderly person with no family," "for a family without health insurance," "for a paralyzed veteran," and several other marginalized individuals. The sentiment is straightforward: Who, among our community's demographic, deserves a financial boost more than those Savinar calls out here?

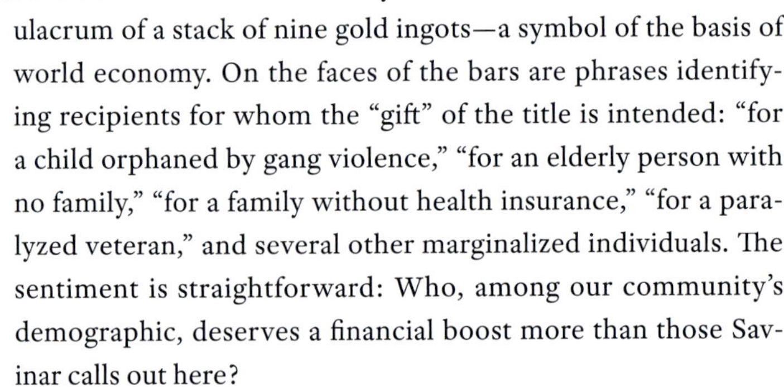

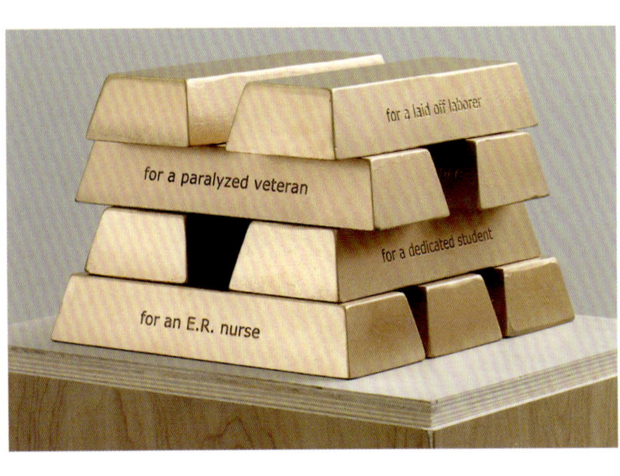

The use of a gold bar as sculpture was first immortalized by the Belgian poet, filmmaker, and artist Marcel Broodthaers

SOME GIFTS

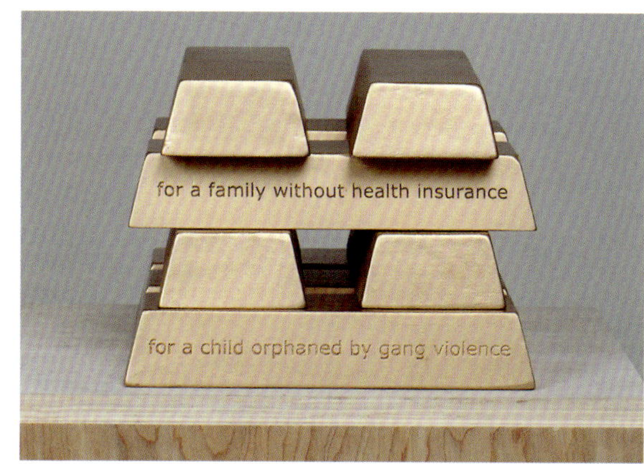

in his conceptual museum, *Museum of Modern Art, Department of Eagles* (1968–71). The "museum" aspect of Broodthaers's project was entirely fictitious, but Broodthaers nonetheless attempted to sell the "museum" on the cover of the 1971 Cologne Art Fair catalogue as follows: "Musée d'Art Moderne à vendre—pour cause de faillite" (Museum of modern art for sale—due to bankruptcy). When the sale failed to allure potential buyers, Broodthaers instead produced an unlimited edition of gold ingots and offered them for sale. The price was determined by doubling the market price of gold; the mark-up was intended to represent the ingots' value as works of art. What Savinar's *Some Gifts* has in common with Broodthaers's *L'Ingot* is that in both sculptures, the ingot symbolizes a form of compensation for something for which no monetary value can be assigned—in Broodthaers's instance, his continued conceptual practice or, more generally, "art"; in the Savinar sculpture, ineffable quotients of health, companionship, comfort, or support.

As early as 1982, Savinar was cognizant of sweeping global paradigm shifts, another leitmotif onto which he turned his laser focus. This was the year of the Falklands Crisis, the ten-week war between Argentina and the United Kingdom. Savinar was inspired to make a twenty-foot wall painting called *Eve*, highlighting the way Americans "consumed" war news via television. The next year, Savinar's pivotal wall painting, *Champ* (1983), and subsequent prints of a graphic map of the United States emblazoned with the word "CHAMP," addressed self-congratulatory American supremacy that correlates to military strategies of the 1970s, '80s and early '90s (culminating with Operation Desert Storm). It is a visual parallel to President George W. Bush's 2003 declaration: "Mission Accomplished."

In 2004 Savinar presented a solo show at Savage Fine Art in Portland that included works that indicated a shift in his worldview. The events of September 11, 2001, have had a major and lasting impact on many contemporary artists, and Savinar is no exception. But the terrorist attack was not the only worldwide upheaval marking the new millennium; Savinar was also

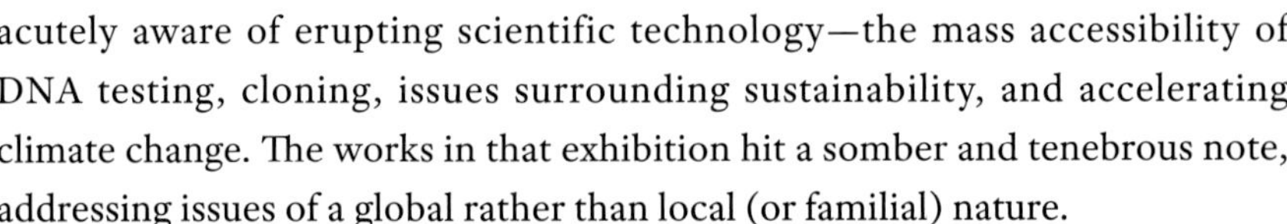

acutely aware of erupting scientific technology—the mass accessibility of DNA testing, cloning, issues surrounding sustainability, and accelerating climate change. The works in that exhibition hit a somber and tenebrous note, addressing issues of a global rather than local (or familial) nature.

The print *Napoleon's MRI* (2004) is a reminder that paradigm shifts can occur elliptically throughout history. The sheet of paper is a lush orchid hue—a little frou-frou, a francophilic nod—but also softly suggesting royal purple. The schematic of a brain is printed in light and dark gray (gray matter); overlaid on the brain is a map of Paris post Napoleon's coup d'état in 1799, around the time that he crowned himself emperor in 1804. Savinar had already used images of brains in previous work—it is a potent illustration for him.[17] The brain is a democratic image[18]—all living beings have one—but, simultaneously, it is as individual as a fingerprint, an understanding we deduce experientially but which is scientifically proven by magnetic resonance imaging (MRI). The inflorescent shape of the brain is a commanding metaphor for creative impulse; the brain also resembles a roiling boil, imitating qualities of extreme individuals—let's say, dictators, such as Napoleon. (The cauliflower-shape of the brain is also mimicked microscopically by some pathogens, like the human papillomavirus, another interesting analogy.) The map of Paris is also ballooning and expanding outward. The print was made during the Iraq War, shortly after the 2003 invasion of Iraq and the toppling of Saddam Hussein's regime. One might view the image of the superimposed map over the brain as an emblem for militaristic strategy and overpowerment. History seems to repeat itself.

NAPOLEON'S MRI (detail)

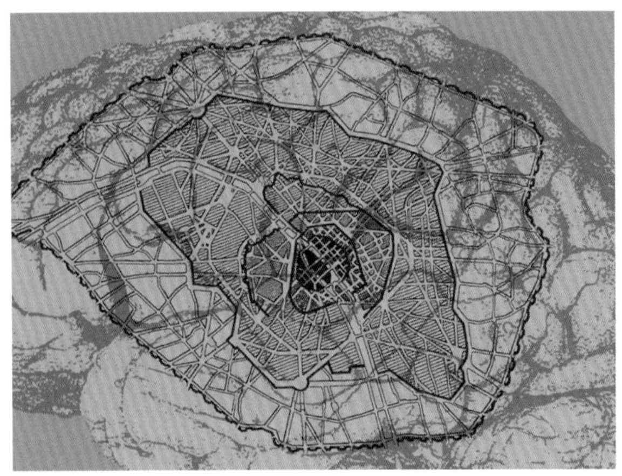

The same exhibition included *News from Tomorrow* (2004), a print whose format and dimensions (5 × 47 inches) mimic television news tickers, such as those that began to be seen at the bottom of the screen on CNN or Fox News.[19] In this print, Savinar again invokes his experience as a playwright, as he anticipates a fictitious future with menacing news bites.

Under "health news," there is the concocted announcement from the American Medical Association calling for the licensing of an urban youth practice

NEWS FROM TOMORROW (details)

called "accessing."[20] In Savinar's made-up ordinance, "accessing" means a "quasi-medical surgical procedure whereby internal organs are made visible through the insertion of a tempered carbide 'window' into the skin of the consumer." Again, Savinar observes culture, then pushes an aspect of it to an exaggerated extreme. Around 2002 Savinar sat in a bar next to a man who attracted his attention. This person had hot-iron-branded tattoos burned into his skin, as well as a pair of silver horns that had been surgically implanted onto his head, like devil horns. This encounter launched Savinar into thinking about other forms of extreme body modification (and there are already many, including transdermal implants, corset piercing, eye-dying, tongue bifurcation, and other surgical alterations). For this component of *News from Tomorrow*, Savinar allowed his imagination to run as far and freely—and even bizarrely—as possible.

In another segment on "consumer news," the ticker announces a holiday shopping incentive to encourage Christmas shoppers to buy early; late "December shoppers" would have to pay a penalty for waiting until the last minute. And in "sports" there is an announcement that the National Football League released a statement discrediting an allegation that live-action broadcasts are computer enhanced for "entertainment"—implying the supposition that one would have a "better" experience watching a sports game on a monitor than in the arena. These, and other news flashes from the future, are humorous—that's one way Savinar lures his viewers into being disposed to participate in a discussion about the arcane nature of contemporary life.

An even more alarming passage from *News from Tomorrow* is this: "The dirty bomb clean-up continues at Disneyland. . . ." The text elicits a horrifying image, but the reality is that twelve years later, during the summer of 2016, a massacre at an Orlando nightclub was committed by a mass murderer who is documented

HEALTH

The American Medical Association called for the licensing of those who practice "accessing." Accessing, the new rage among the urban youth culture, is a quasi-medical surgical procedure whereby internal organs are made visible through the insertion of a tempered carbide "window" into the skin of the consumer. Currently, this procedure is practiced primarily by cosmeticians and has not required parental permission for those under the age of eighteen.

CONSUMER NEWS

Last-minute Christmas shoppers beware. In a novel approach to boost holiday sales, the National Retailers Association of America announced today that they will divide the holiday shopping season into two purchasing opportunities. The first period will stretch from October 1 to November 30 and the second from December 1 to December 26. During the December period shoppers will need to purchase a "Preferred Late Shopper Card" in order to gain access to stores. Only those holding cards will be permitted to shop during the month of December. Cards will cost $350, are only good for one holiday season, and may be obtained at any Gold Level Signature One Premier Starbucks location.

NATIONAL

The dirty bomb clean-up continues at Disneyland in Anaheim. Although Disneyland officials have said they intend to re-build the park, it is still unclear if it will be undertaken at the park's original location.

In related news, a spokesperson for the families of the victims announced today that a memorial is in the planning stages with an open international design competition set to begin in December.

THE LAST MOMENTS PRECEDING THE DEATH OF CIVILITY (detail)

as having considered staging his terrorist act at Disney World. All of a sudden, the unthinkable is conceivable.

Savinar relentlessly scrutinizes the world around him and uses his sharp observations as source material. "In much of my work I often observe some event or behavior and ask myself what might happen if this thing continues on into the future, or what an exaggerated notion of this thing might be," Savinar says. "I feel that by exaggerating or magnifying something and presenting it to my viewer, they will scoff at it as hyperbole. How might I exaggerate it into the future in order to have the viewer consider the present behavior absurd? This, of course, encourages them to assess the current state of affairs."

This sort of stylistic parable is not unique to Savinar—most famously, many comparisons have been made between George Orwell's *1984* and the present day. Perhaps the whole world has not devolved into a totalitarian state, but the Big Brother concepts spun by Orwell in his 1949 novel bear a striking resemblance to our National Security Agency's warrantless wire-tapping call database (MARINA) and data-mining (PRISM). Or, in theater, an art form so closely associated with Savinar's creative output, Thornton Wilder's 1942 Pulitzer Prize–winning play, *The Skin of Our Teeth*, spins a pre-absurdist family epic that predicts global warming, perpetual series of wars, the insanity of conventions and elections, and increasingly endangered and extinct species—all of which are exploding present-day threats. These are just two examples in a long history of artists assuming the role of the proverbial canary in the coal mine.

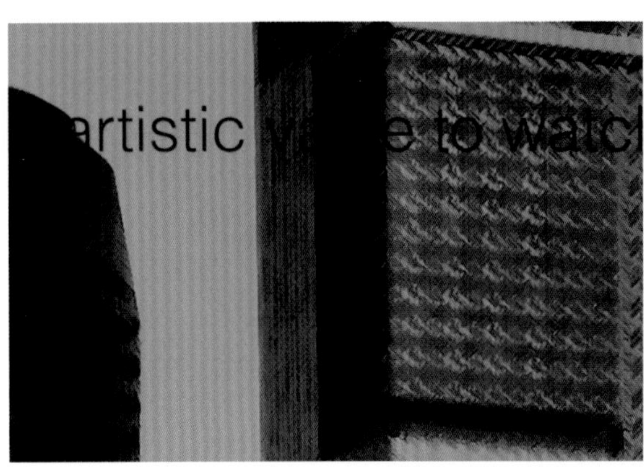

The Last Moments Preceding the Death of Civility (2004) is yet another commentary on social, political, and pop culture in which Savinar observes, then hyperbolizes. This is an ominous print illustrating a cityscape illuminated by the light of late afternoon; the glow dissolves into near-dusk and eventual total blackness, as if the sun has just permanently set on decorum. For this image, Savinar worked side by side with an architect to design an ensemble of

THE LAST MOMENTS PRECEDING THE DEATH OF CIVILITY (detail)

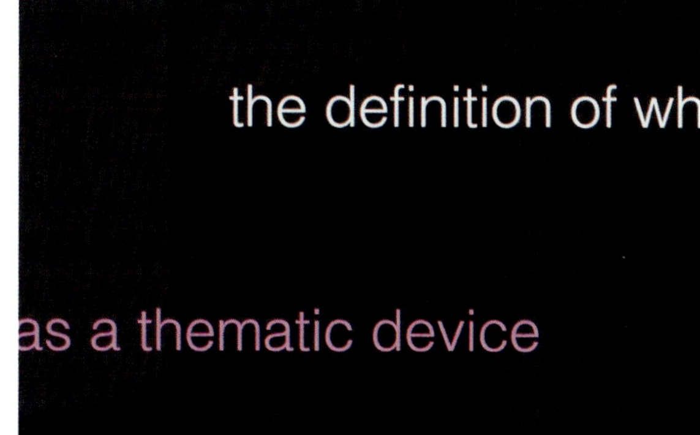

skyscrapers, amalgamated to look like an every-city, but not a specific, identifiable urban core.

The overlaid text lists (laterally, from left to right, similar to *News from Tomorrow*) "symptoms" denoting the death of civility in order of perceived severity. In 2004, when this image was made, relatively benign lapses in collective common sense included citations such as "un-neighborly leaf blower use," "anti-social jaywalking," and the names of then-current pop icons "Britney, Paris, et al."[21] The furthest along in the print's timeline, before the viewer reaches far right edge, is the final signifier of the death of civility: "televised decapitations." From the present perspective, civility has already died.

At the time of Savinar's making of *Death of Civility*, the idea of a televised decapitation was still incogitable, although it had occurred. It was in 2002 that the *Wall Street Journal* reporter Daniel Pearl was abducted by Islamic militants and eventually murdered. On February 21, 2002, the kidnappers released a videotape titled *The Slaughter of the Spy-Journalist, the Jew Daniel Pearl*; in the span of three minutes, thirty-six seconds, Pearl was seen making forced propaganda statements, his throat was slit, and his head was severed—the first graphic video of a human decapitation to be circulated on the Internet. Within a couple of months, the *Boston Phoenix* published a link to the video from their website, spawning an outcry of protest for "callous disregard for human decency."[22]

Only two years later—the same year that the Savinar image was made—the American engineer Nick Berg was kidnapped and then killed on videotape. This time, Reuters made the unedited video available within days; all major US television news networks showed the clip, stopping short of broadcasting the beheading itself. Within a day of its release, the top ten Internet search terms included references to Nick Berg. In 2004 there were sixty-four documented beheadings in Iraq; twenty-eight were filmed. A Dutch website owner reported that daily viewing numbers spiked from 300,000 to 750,000 when a decapitation video was released from Iraq.

H5N1 VIRUS CENTRAL LIBRARY DISTRIBUTION PAD (detail)

OCCURRENCES (detail)

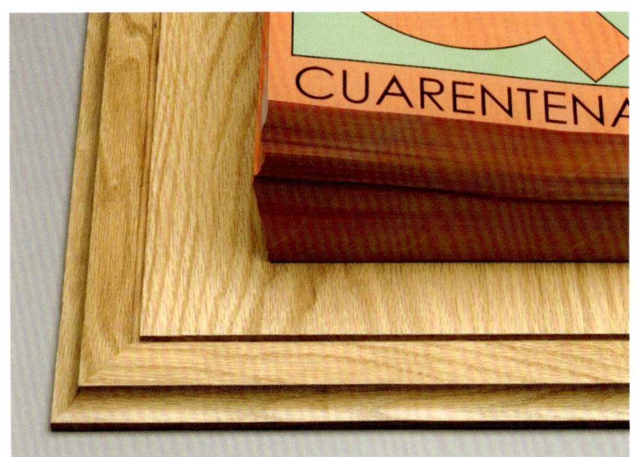

It is an eerie fact of Savinar's oeuvre that he has a history of focusing on a trend or event that, at the time of its making, seems preposterous or absurd—but then, in ensuing years, comes to be reality. His concept for *Talk Radio* predated the conservative Rush Limbaugh's first show in 1984, syndicated nationally in 1988. *Cover Shot* (1989), his play about celebrity starchitects designing ego museums, long predated Frank Gehry's Bilbao (1997), Daniel Libeskind's Jewish Museum, Berlin (1999), or Renzo Piano's addition to the Art Institute of Chicago (2009).

There are scarier examples, too. Savinar's sculpture *H5N1 Virus Central Library Distribution Pad* (2006) is a hypothetical paper pad to provide warnings to be placed in home windows. The piece consists of a pad of tear-off sheets of paper emblazoned with a graphic "Q" in bright orange against lime green with text that says "quarantine/cuarentena." The idea is that stacks of these signs could be located in libraries or other community centers, for citizens to take home a warning against avian influenza. The piece is sort of funny, in a ludicrous way—what a great public service! Handy government-issued quarantine signs! But it is sobering to remember that the H1N1 virus was responsible for the swine flu pandemic of 2009, three years after Savinar conceived this sculpture. And then it was only in mid-2016 that the World Health Organization declared the end of the Ebola virus transmission in West Africa, which started in 2014.

DEVELOPMENT PROJECTS.

6. 40.000 PEOPLE A YEAR DIE FROM AIR POLLU

1. China 2014
2. Rome 2014
3. America 2014
4. India 2014
5. America 2014
6. Paris 2005

In Savinar's hands, though, the idea that he takes something to its logical—or, rather, *il*logical extension, only to have it come forth in documented truth—seems to span a more condensed, quickened timeframe.

In 2013 Savinar mounted an exhibition at his gallery, PDX Contemporary in Portland. It was only in unpacking his work to install on the gallery walls that Savinar made a sobering discovery. To his surprise, in the entire show, not one of his works included language. It was as if Savinar were "speechless," or had "nothing to say." This experience catapulted him into a self-designed

EVERYTHING IS BROKEN (detail)

sabbatical of sorts; he went to Florence, Italy, for an extended stay. He procured a studio there, but his intentions for using it were more along the lines of giving himself space to reflect on his visual art career. Instead, his months in Florence launched a motherlode of new and compelling material.

Savinar would sit at a Florentine café, drinking his morning cappuccinos, reading the *International Herald Tribune*, noticing the alarming news items from around the globe. *Occurrences* (2014) is a list—a trope that Savinar uses repeatedly—where the *il*logical has already become fact. There are six items on the list, all of them a bit dystopian, statements that seem unbelievable, but that also have the ring of authority of cold, hard statistics. "Children upon reaching the age of five shall be transferred by their parents to private or state-run boarding kindergartens," or "Extensive tracts of land included within national park lands shall be sold to the private sector for new development projects," or "Newborn infants will arrive with 100% immunity to the effectiveness of all existing antibiotics. Due to fears of adversely impacting the highly profitable medical tourism industry, all further research into combating infant diseases will be curtailed." These preposterous sound bites feel like science fiction but, in fact, at the bottom of the list is a red box, a list within the list: it documents the country or city and year in which each of these unthinkable events has already come to pass. Savinar could not have known, with certainty, that in the year following *Occurrences*, the United States Senate would vote 51 to 49 to support an amendment for budget resolution enabling the government to sell all federal lands.[23] The measure, if implemented, will put hundreds of millions of acres of national forests, rangelands, wildlife refuges, wilderness areas, and historic sites up for sale.

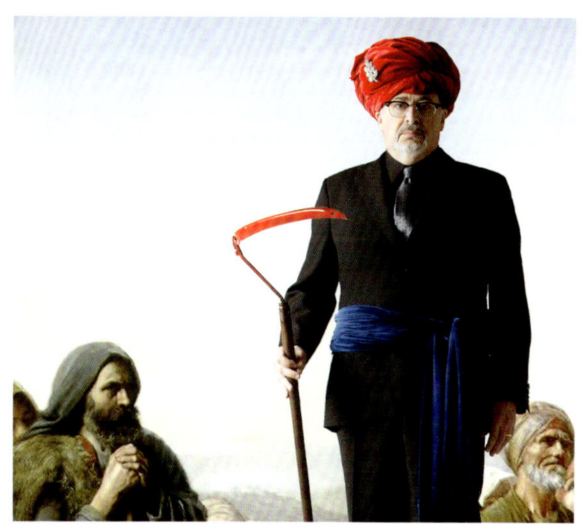

The dominant image in *Everything Is Broken* (2014) is a digitally altered reproduction of *Sermon on the Mount* (1877), a painting by Carl Heinrich Bloch,[24] a nineteenth-century Danish genre painter whose work helped to establish a Western aesthetic celebrating daily life. Superimposed onto the rock in Bloch's painting from which Christ is preaching is an awkward full-frontal self-portrait of Savinar, slightly smaller than the rest of the human figures,

EVERYTHING IS BROKEN (detail)

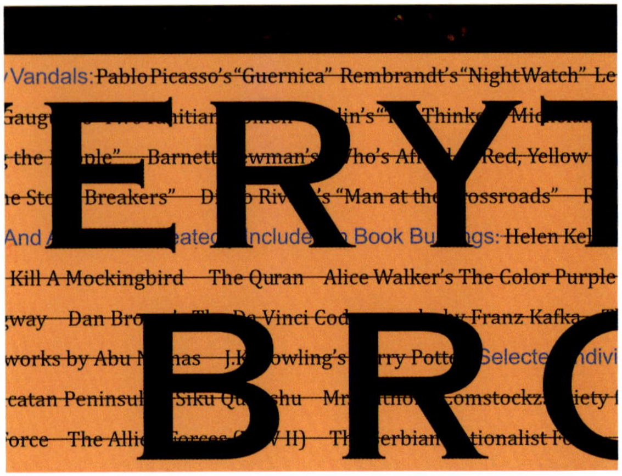

dressed in a contemporary dark suit, wearing a blue sash with gold tassels and a red turban[25] in a kind of mashed-up costume.[26] The artist holds a scythe in his hands—a powerful symbol of death (as in the Grim Reaper), but also a representation of the passage of time (as in a tool of harvest) and a morality icon—"whatever you sow so shall you reap." But Savinar is quick to remind us that he is talking to the viewer, not the historian. The impact of the imposition of Savinar's self-portrait should be its visceral content.

Below the digitized alteration of the Bloch *Sermon on the Mount* is a band of categories listing "selected works of art that have been damaged by vandals," "selected works of literature and authors repeatedly included in book burnings," "selected individuals who set fire to libraries or staged significant public book burnings," and "selected significant libraries set on fire," along with a long list of specific examples. Shockingly included are paintings such as Rembrandt's *The Night Watch*, Rodin's *The Thinker*, and Courbet's *The Stone Breakers*, and beloved literary classics, like Harper Lee's *To Kill a Mockingbird*, along with J. K. Rowling's *Harry Potter*, the Talmud, the Bible, and the Quran. Superimposed over the lengthy tally of destruction are the words "Everything Is Broken," as if the cycle of creative output and censorship is condemned to eternal repetition.

It is gripping to realize that Savinar conceived this work in Florence; his studio, a mere three blocks from the site where Fra Girolamo Savonarola conducted the Bonfires of the Vanities (in fact, the cleric even convinced Italian Renaissance masters such as Sandro Botticelli and Lorenzo di Credi to publically destroy their own paintings). It is uncanny, too, that the names "Savinar" and "Savonarola" are virtually alliterate. And, in another, deeper parallel, Savinar went to Florence with the intention that, in a careful review of his career, he might very well be "burning" it. Instead, Savinar's pilgrimage resurrected it.

The Savinar self-portrait underscores yet another subtext in *Everything Is Broken*. Here the artist implicates *himself* as both a thief and a vandal. After all, he appropriated the historic painting by Bloch, then defaced it by inserting his own likeness into the picture. It is an amplification, of course, but the

2064: ENGLAND'S MASTER ARCHITECT... (details)

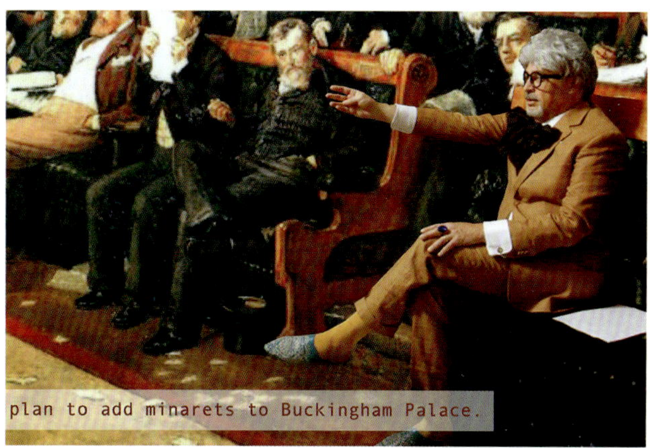

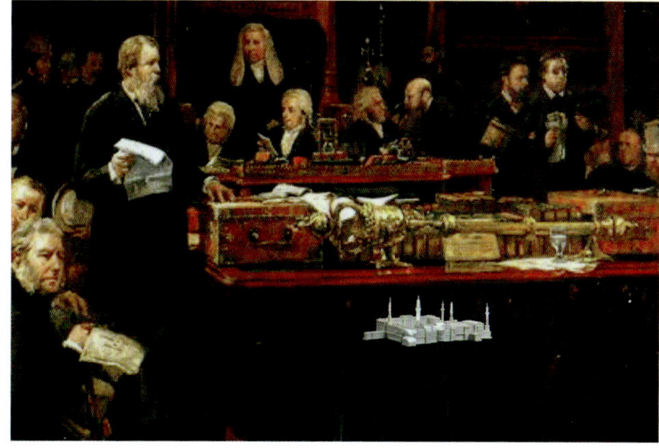

point is clear that there are elements of the past, present, and even future desecration implied by this image. In fact, by the year following the making of this print, ISIS deliberately and even exuberantly destroyed the ancient Syrian city of Palmyra, a UNESCO World Heritage Site considered to be one of the best-preserved sites from antiquity for the past 1,500 years. The irrevocable obliteration of the Palmyra ruins proves Savinar's point that cycles of expurgation will not end anytime soon.

And then there is the print *2064: England's Master Architect Presents, to the House of Commons, the Plan to Add Minarets to Buckingham Palace* (2014). At first viewing, the image seems a little coy. It looks like a reproduction of a nineteenth-century history painting, William Morrison Wyllie's *The House of Commons* (1878).[27] On closer inspection, the viewer realizes that the painting has been digitally altered. In front of the despatch box, the lectern from which members of Parliament deliver speeches to their parliamentary chamber, there is an architectural model of Buckingham Palace with minarets. The idea that minarets might be architecturally added to the official residence of the British royal family implies that a cross-marriage has created change in the nobility. Worry over a royal marrying a commoner has been replaced with the consequences of the Church of England running headlong into Islam.

On the far right side of the image Savinar includes a self-portrait in a powdered wig, wearing a foppish cravat, French cuffs, and a huge ring on his left-hand middle finger. He is also sporting bright-blue embroidered Turkish slippers, a signifier that, by the fictitious year 2064, it is estimated that the majority of Britons will be Muslim. Eastern fashion has now become mainstream in the West. As the self-appointed "Master Architect," Savinar is pointing to the model as if describing the details to Parliament. In terms of artistic augury, it is interesting to note that in 2016, Londoners elected as mayor Sadiq

THE NEW MAN (detail)

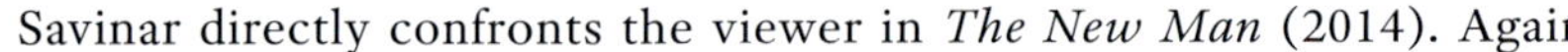

Khan, a Muslim Zionist, after a contentious campaign, two years *after* Savinar conceived the image.

Savinar directly confronts the viewer in *The New Man* (2014). Again inspired by his time in Florence, Savinar appropriated a painting by the Netherlandish artist Quentin Metsys, *Portrait of a Canon* (before 1523),[28] and altered it into a cheeky self-portrait. The sitter is featured half-length, seated behind a table, typical of a traditional Renaissance portrait. He is wearing an elaborate costume, designed to approximate the Metsys portrait: a black undergarment, heavy surplice with fur cuffs, an embroidered kufi. The accoutrements in the foreground also reference the Metsys. Savinar holds spectacles in his heavily ringed right hand, and in his left hand, instead of a book, he grasps an iPad. Also before Savinar is a striped porcelain teacup, an Italian heirloom of his grandmother's—remember, Savinar does not shy away from sentimentality. This is a tableau redolent of intellect, achievement, confidence.

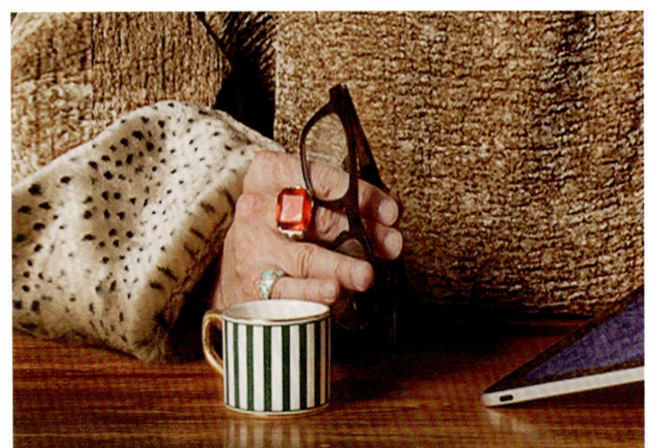

The effort that went into the making of this picture is another example of the artist's obsessiveness, as well as his debt to theater. Savinar recounts a story of his delight in, say, finding the *perfect* fountain pen to place in the pocket of a character in one of his plays. Even though the pen is never removed from the pocket, only an inch or so of the pen shows above the pocket edge, and the audience that experiences the character is fifty feet away, the pinnacle of attention to detail is meaningful to Savinar, and he strives to achieve it in every work. He likens it to "the hunt," and it is a part of his art-making process that he relishes.

If Savinar seeks to generate a sincere back-and-forth conversation with his viewer, *The New Man* is formally composed to do so. The figure's gaze is straightforward as it meets the viewer; he looks like he is about to start an important meeting. Again, Savinar has invoked humor and chutzpah to engage the viewer; once the viewer is drawn in, the conversation can begin. But what is the underlying message in this image? That the sitter is Savinar himself—that shock of recognition—immediately arrests a viewer who knows the artist: this scene is taking place here and now; it's not an anonymous or theoretical act. For viewers who do not know Savinar, there is still the sense that the sitter is a person in real time, therefore underscoring the urgency of Savinar's message. The aesthetic may invoke the luxuriance of the Renaissance, and there is the subtext that "the artist" is royalty, but both of those ideas stand in stark contrast to the reality of today's world.

These latest prints by Savinar leave us lingering in Florence, the city-shrine to the Renaissance and the fountainhead of ideas, concepts, and images that currently occupy this artist. Surrounded by the history of thousands of years, Savinar found himself ogling the ferocious future, and wondering if humanity has learned any significant lessons over the past many centuries. Invoking beauty, language, content, and irony, Savinar's elemental quartet, the viewer joins the artist in a conversation with no end.

NOTES

1.
Carlo McCormick, "West of Here: Ed Ruscha at the De Young Museum," *Juxtapoz*, no. 187 (August 2016), 51.

2.
Bernard Blistène, "Conversation with Ed Ruscha," *Edward Ruscha: Paintings=Schilderijen*, exh. cat. (Rotterdam: Museum Boijmans Van Beuningen, 1989), 134.

3.
Savinar was introduced to Joe Brainard's work by fellow artist Bill Hoppe.

4.
Joe Brainard, *I Remember* (New York: Full Court Press, 1975), 39.

5.
Ibid., 31.

6.
Ibid., 72

7.
As reprinted on www.joebrainard.org.

8.
Another similarity between Brainard and Savinar is their use of the pronoun "I," a purposeful and effective choice to pull in the reader/viewer.

9.
The collaboration was supported by a National Endowment for the Arts Inter-Arts Program grant and a Metropolitan Arts Commission (now Regional Arts and Culture Council) grant. The play, cocreated by Tad Savinar and Eric Bogosian and written by Eric Bogosian, premiered at PCVA in 1985 and went on to be produced at the Public Theater, New York City in 1987; eventually, the film rights were purchased and Oliver Stone directed a movie based on the play (1988). *Talk Radio* was nominated for a Pulitzer Prize in 1985 and then, when it played on Broadway in 2007, it received two Tony nominations.

10.
The work of artist Annette Lemieux (b. 1957) also deeply resonated with Savinar.

11.
After his collaboration with Bogosian, Savinar wrote the following plays: *Autoflex* (1986, Portland Center for the Visual Arts and Portland Civic Theatre); *Re-wired* (1986, Commissioned and produced by Portland Civic Theatre); *Brushfires: A Biased View of Power in the West* (1986, Portland Civic Theatre); *The 4 Mickies* (1988, Artist Repertory Theater, Portland); *Cover Shot* (1990, commissioned by the Oregon Shakespeare Festival, Portland, and first performed in a full production by the Portland Repertory Theater in 1994).

12.
Mother's Pride (1998, acrylic on canvas with copper tag, 22.5 × 14.75 inches) is based on a painting of a ewe and her lamb made by Sean Cain, commissioned by Savinar.

13.
A Christian legend associated with lily of the valley is that when the Virgin Mary wept over the Crucifixion of her son, her tears turned into lilies of the valley, thereby lending the term "Mary's Tears" as another common name for this plant. This symbolism is the opposite of purity and innocence; it suggests sacrifice and heartbreak, which are also sometimes part of the parenthood experience.

14.
Another hallmark of Savinar's career, not discussed here, is a long list of civic memorials that he has designed or on which he has collaborated. These include conceptual designs for the Oregon Holocaust Memorial (1996), Columbine High School Memorial (1999), and the New Jersey State WW II Memorial (2001). An important print reflective of Savinar's involvement in civic memorials is *Hope* (2008), a departure from other prints in his oeuvre because the print is devoid of image, except for black text on gray paper. The print recounts an experience—a reaction—to being deeply steeped in the human sadness that precedes the need for memorialization.

15.
In Savinar's play, the plotline revolves around an architect who closely resembles Michael Graves and the fictitious architect's son, who closely resembles Peter Eisenman.

16.
Development was made just one year after the Portland Art Museum renovated the Masonic Temple adjacent to the Pietro Belluschi building that originally housed the museum. In the flurry to raise the largest capital sum ever amassed by a cultural organization in the state of Oregon, the lengths to which the museum went to generate "naming opportunities" were nearly comical—and resulted in situations where formerly named components were *re*-named.

17.
Savinar's other works involving the brain image include the drawings *Left Brains/Right Brains* (2003) and the sculpture *Human ~~Kind~~* (2004).

18.
Napoleon's reign is fraught with paradoxical and opposing examples of how he either betrayed the higher ideals of the French Revolution, retarding democratic progress, or propelled French government toward a more egalitarian state than the country experienced under the crown. Savinar's choice of Napoleon as a world leader is, as always, deliberate and deeply considered.

19.
Television "tickers" hark back to paper ticker tape, the earliest digital electronics communication medium, once used to transmit stock price information over telegraph lines. Paper ticker tape has been obsolete since the 1960s.

20.
This term and definition were entirely made up by Savinar.

21.
Future viewers will likely recognize the name Britney Spears—in 2003 her fourth studio album, *In the Zone*, was listed by NPR as one of "The 50 Most Important Recordings of the Decade" and her career has continued to flourish—but the reference to "Paris," as in celebrity socialite Paris Hilton will have likely outlived its fame. If this work were made today, perhaps "Kim" Kardashian and "Kanye" West might have been cited instead.

22.
http://www.salon.com/2015/02/03/what_a_beheading_feels_like_the_science_the_gruesome_spectacle_and_why_we_cant_look_away/

23.
In the case of this amendment, national parks and monuments are not included. Will Rogers, "Our Land, Up for Grabs," *New York Times*, April 2, 2015.

24.
Source material for this print is Carl Heinrich Bloch (1834–1890), *Sermon on the Mount*, 1877, oil on copper, 40.9 × 36.2 inches; located at the Museum of National History at Frederiksborg Castle, Denmark. For more than forty years, the Church of Jesus Christ of Latter-Day Saints has heavily reproduced Bloch's paintings of the life of Christ in print and electronic marketing materials.

25.
According to the website www.raqs.co.nz, a turban color signifies specific attributes. According to this source, a red turban designates the wearer as a Samaritan. In the case of Savinar's *Everything Is Broken*, one could interpret Savinar—or "the artist"—as "Good Samaritan," preserving culture instead of obliterating it. The red turban is also a reference to Jan van Eyck's *Portrait of a Man* (1433, National Gallery, London). But Savinar states that there was no symbolism intended in the costume of this self-portrait, other than to invoke an amalgam of Western, Turkish, Indian, and even Mafia "fashion."

26.
Savinar has used his own portrait in his work dating back to the 1970s, even though most of his experimentations with self-portraiture were never widely exhibited. Not only was he influenced in this by his participation in theater, but he was also reacting to the presence of performance art, both nationally (Vito Acconci) and locally (Paul Sutinen). In the late 1970s, Savinar even had a "clean room" in his apartment, in which he was able to photograph his constructions; he often included himself in the photo documentation in a performative or theatrical manner.

27.
Source material for this print is William Morrison Wyllie (c. 1820–1895), *The House of Commons*, 1878, oil on canvas, 30 × 50 in.; in the Parliamentary Art Collection.

28.
Source material for this print is Quentin Metsys (1466–1530), *Portrait of a Canon*, before 1523, oil on panel, 29 × 23.5 in.; located at the Palais Liechtenstein, Vienna.

Biography

Tad Savinar was born in Portland, Oregon, in 1950 and received a bachelor of arts degree in studio art from Colorado College in 1973. One-person or significant installations of his work have occurred at such institutions as the New Museum and Artists Space, New York; Los Angeles Institute of Contemporary Art (LAICA); Atlanta Contemporary; Center on Contemporary Art (COCA), Seattle; Portland Art Museum, Portland Center for the Visual Arts (PCVA); and The Art Gym at Marylhurst University, Portland. Savinar's works are included in the collections of the Museum of Modern Art, New York; the Smithsonian Institution Archives in Washington, DC; the Fabric Workshop and Museum in Philadelphia; the Norton Museum of Art, Miami; Portland Art Museum; and the Art, Design & Architecture Museum, University of California, Santa Barbara.

Savinar has been the recipient of three National Endowment for the Arts Fellowships in addition to other regional fellowships. In 1998 he was awarded the Oregon Governor's Arts Award.

He is currently represented by PDX Contemporary Gallery in Portland.

Artist's Acknowledgments

I especially wish to acknowledge that since I set up a studio in 1973, Jordan Schnitzer has acted as an extraordinary patron of my work. However, he is no ordinary patron, for he has often also served as my muse and even at times as my toughest critic.

I first began speaking with Linda Tesner, the director of the Ronna and Eric Hoffman Gallery of Contemporary Art at Lewis & Clark College, in 2015. Through multiple conversations we conceived the exhibition *youniverse—past, present, future* and ultimately this book in 2016. It was in those discussions that I found her limitless enthusiasm and encyclopedic ability to connect the dots between social cultures and art historical cultures so compelling. Her insights, her questions, and her resulting essay will, I hope, provide the reader with a new lens to engage with my work. I am deeply indebted to her for this gift at this milestone in my career.

Funding for the *youniverse* exhibition was provided by generous support from The Ford Family Foundation, the Oregon Arts Commission, Jordan D. Schnitzer, and Lewis & Clark College—all of whom help to foster a rich cultural community in which contemporary art is made accessible to all.

Lucia|Marquand accepted my challenge of designing a book that was easy to hold in one's hand, eminently readable, and contemporary in feel—and ran with it. The book is indeed a testament to their ability to translate my desires.

Tad Savinar

Director's Acknowledgments

The Ronna and Eric Hoffman Gallery of Contemporary Art at Lewis & Clark College is pleased to publish this volume on the occasion of the exhibition *youniverse—past, present, future: Selected Works by Tad Savinar from the Jordan D. Schnitzer Collection* (January 17–March 5, 2017). Tad Savinar has been a practicing studio artist for over four decades, contributing to the visual landscape through work that is socially complex and responsive to our time. Thank you to Tad for producing work that is both conceptually contemplative and beautiful to view.

The exhibition, *youniverse—past, present, future,* was made possible by the generosity of Jordan D. Schnitzer, who loaned almost all of the works in the exhibition. Mr. Schnitzer is a dedicated collector who has acquired a comprehensive body of work representing Savinar's long career. Thank you to Jordan for his commitment to this artist and for his support of the exhibition.

This book, *Pictures that Talk*, was made possible by a generous grant from The Ford Family Foundation. The Ford Family Foundation is a leader in its support of Oregon artists and, through its support of scholarship and documentation, contributes to the preservation of Oregon's art ecology and visual art history. Lewis & Clark College is indebted to The Ford Family Foundation and, in particular, to Carol Dalu and Kandis Brewer Nunn.

Linda Tesner

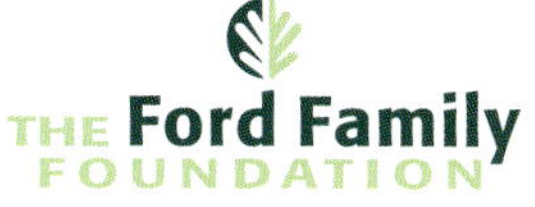